A CITY OF IMAGES

A City of Images

ICONOGRAPHY AND SOCIETY IN ANCIENT GREECE

by

CLAUDE BÉRARD, CHRISTIANE BRON,

JEAN-LOUIS DURAND, FRANÇOISE FRONTISI-DUCROUX,

FRANÇOIS LISSARRAGUE, ALAIN SCHNAPP, AND

JEAN-PIERRE VERNANT

Translated by

DEBORAH LYONS

PRINCETON, NEW JERSEY
PRINCETON UNIVERSITY PRESS
MCM · LXXXIX

COPYRIGHT © 1989 BY PRINCETON UNIVERSITY PRESS
PUBLISHED BY PRINCETON UNIVERSITY PRESS, 41 WILLIAM STREET
PRINCETON, NEW JERSEY 08540
IN THE UNITED KINGDOM:
PRINCETON UNIVERSITY PRESS, GUILDFORD, SURREY

LIBRARY OF CONGRESS CATALOGING IN PUBLICATION
DATA WILL BE FOUND ON THE LAST PRINTED PAGE OF THIS BOOK
ISBN 0-691-03591-1
THIS BOOK HAS BEEN COMPOSED IN TIMES NEW ROMAN

CLOTHBOUND EDITIONS OF PRINCETON UNIVERSITY
PRESS BOOKS ARE PRINTED ON ACID-FREE
PAPER, AND BINDING MATERIALS
ARE CHOSEN FOR STRENGTH
AND DURABILITY

*

PRINTED IN LAUSANNE, SWITZERLAND, BY
BRON SA AU MONT-SUR-LAUSANNE

CONTENTS

Preface

JEAN-PIERRE VERNANT

The authors of this book invite us to explore with them the exotic and distant world of Greek culture, through the imagery of Attic vases of the sixth and fifth centuries. Page by page, they lead us by the hand, seeking to make this distant world more familiar to us. In so doing, they have not only assembled some of the most beautiful images ever made; their wish has been to make them speak to us. They have tried, as far as possible, to restore to us the message that the artisans of the Kerameikos, who inscribed these precious decorations on the sides of a fine piece of pottery, meant to communicate to those who would use the vessel in their daily lives, display it in their houses, bury it in their tombs, and export it far across the entire Mediterranean. For this pottery is as much an expression of the creative genius of Athens as the works of its poets, playwrights, orators, and philosophers.

This book, conceived by Hellenists—archaeologists, historians, philologists—is addressed to a wider audience, beyond the circle of specialists. Its aim is to make accessible to this audience a human universe now vanished, a sunken continent of which nothing remains to evoke its extraordinary richness but written texts and pictorial documents, most often taken out of a fragmented archaeological context. Neither kind of document is immediately transparent. To understand them, one must, in the course of a long apprenticeship, internalize the techniques that allow us to decipher them. To read one of these texts presupposes that one has gradually learned to think like a Greek, using the intellectual categories and the mental framework that were theirs. To read one of these images also implies learning to see like a Greek, struggling to penetrate the visual code that made these various images immediately readable to contemporary eyes.

Since we belong to a civilization of the book, of writing and reading, it is the texts that up until now have been the main object of scholarly research and interpretation. Hence the overly literary idea of the ancient world, and of Athens in particular, that classical studies have presented. In the last few years, however, we have come to realize the great importance of imagery in certain cultures, and above all the specificity of the language of the plastic arts, which has its particular aims, its norms and requirements, its own means of expression and communication. At the same time, Hellenists have encountered, outside their own traditional disciplines, the contributions of anthropologists and semioticians, which they have had to take into account as they approach and examine ancient civilization.

Two concerns have thus shaped the collective work of the team of researchers involved in *The City of Images*. In the first place, they have begun by making a selection from among the mass of pictorial documents. Leaving aside the numerous mythological scenes, many justly famous, they have retained those series of images, grouped about major anthropological themes—the youth, the warrior, women, domestic and wild animals in their relation to human beings, the erotic, 7 the religious festival, the Dionysiac world—which project a strong light on some of the most pronounced traits of what one might call the social construction of reality of classical Athens, the way it functions, the figures it privileges, and those it rejects, the scenes it highlights and those it leaves in shadow, the classifications created by the interplay of connections and oppositions, as well as by the displacements, the shifts and sometimes blurrings between different categories of images.

Secondly, it was the authors' intention that the presentation and interpretation of the images, intimately related, progress together in each chapter, so that the commentary never strays far from the figural field, but always takes its support exclusively from the vocabulary of pictorial language, its repertoire of forms, the composition of its scenes, the internal logic of the system.

This project, ambitious and new as it is, is in no way definitive or dogmatic. The authors, instead, emphasize the difficulties, the obstacles, the necessary uncertainties of deciphering. In so doing, they stress a fundamental point, that no figurative system is constituted as a simple illustration of discourse, oral or written, nor as an exact photographic reproduction of reality. The imagery is a construct, not a carbon copy; it is a work of culture, the creation of a language that like all other languages contains an essential element of arbitrariness. The repertoire of figural forms that each civilization elaborates and organizes after its own fashion, in its own style, wherever it chooses, seems always to be the product of a filtering, framing, or encoding of reality according to the modes of thought native to that civilization.

It is this social arbitrariness that explains the difficulties of deciphering the images, and at the same time justifies their use as a means to grasp the specific traits of a culture. I would also emphasize among the lessons one may take away from this book, that which seems to me to concern us the most directly. The authors, inviting us to look through the lens of Greek imagery and to reject intuitive and obvious naturalistic interpretations of figural representations, force us to reexamine our own social constructs. But this detour through Greek imagery brings us back to a source of these constructs, and by demonstrating their cultural relativity, not only strips them of the authority they have assumed, but also throws them into sharper relief.

A CITY OF IMAGES

FIG. I. *Athena, goddess of technical intelligence, crowns the potter.*

CHAPTER I

Looking at the Vase

CHRISTIANE BRON AND
FRANÇOIS LISSARRAGUE

The Kerameikos is the name given the potters' quarter in Athens, located near the cemetery. In the eighth century, the workshops of this quarter provided the large geometric vases used as funerary monuments. It is on these vases that figurative representations—battle scenes and funeral processions—make their first appearance. During the seventh and sixth centuries, the artists of the Kerameikos imitated the Corinthian style of pottery, but in the mid-sixth century they created a style of their own which was to be tremendously successful throughout the Mediterranean down to the beginning of the fourth century. For almost one hundred and fifty years, potters and painters worked not only for their own city, but for many foreign customers as well, especially from Etruria and Southern Italy.

Unfortunately, we know very little about how these workshops functioned. The few depictions on vases suggest that artisans worked collectively, but we have only imprecise knowledge about the links between potters and painters, between the head of a studio and his assistants, as well as the way in which subject matter and motifs were transmitted. Some potters' signatures allow us to suppose familial continuity within a workshop, while others indicate that a single vase was made and decorated by two different hands.

Whenever a painter does depict his workshop, it is to show Athena, the goddess of technical skill, at the side of the craftsmen, who are empowered by her presence to carry out successfully the delicate operations of turning, decorating, and firing the vase.

Numerous risks, including warpage, cracking due to shrinkage, and misfiring, stand in the way of successful completion of the painted vase. In figure 1, we see two representations of Nike, the symbol of success, helping Athena to crown craftsmen who are decorating kraters and kantharoi. On the far right, a woman paints the volute of a large krater. Whether a slave or a free woman, her presence indicates an area of feminine activity quite different from the traditional tasks of the gynaeceum.

In the sixth century, the vases are decorated with images incised and painted in black glaze heightened with white or purple on the red ground of the clay. This technique, known as "black-figure," is superceded around 520 by the inverse technique of "red-figure," in which the glazed background shows as black and the red figures are reserved. From this point on, it is no longer necessary to incise the anatomical details, which are now painted with a much more supple line, either in thick black or in the lighter brown obtained with dilute glaze, allowing for a subtler drawing technique and more precise modeling.

This new product seems to have enjoyed considerable success, judging from the numerous finds of Attic pottery from Spain to the Black Sea, from Gaul to Egypt. It is to Etruscan funeral practices, however, that our current knowledge of Greek vases owes its greatest debt. These status symbols, imported from Athens, were placed along with bronze objects, necklaces, and other jewelry, in Etruscan chamber-tombs, built like underground houses. In these tombs, they were preserved intact until their discovery beginning in the late 18th century.

Beyond their exotic and elegant character, what made them precious to the Etruscans—as they are to us—was their figurative decoration, as we see from the ancient imitations produced by Etruscan craftsmen. Attic pottery offers a tremendous iconographic richness. Few ancient cultures have provided us with a repertory of images equal to the one through which we hope to lead the reader in the course of this volume. Since we have elected to omit discussion of vase shapes in the following chapters, we will present here a brief overview by way of preface.

FIG. 2. *The vase has a body whose different parts are described metaphorically in our vocabulary.*

FIG. 3. *Metaphor becomes reality as genitals replace the foot of a cup.*

In the hands of the potter, the vase resembles a body to which he gives shape. Our vocabulary describes the anatomy of the vase metaphorically, speaking of its neck, belly, shoulder, foot, and lip (fig. 2). The Greeks themselves spoke of the head of the vase, of its face (prosopon) to designate the inside of a cup, and of ears for its handles. The vase has a mouth (stoma), a belly (gaster), and sometimes even a navel (omphalos, fig. 99).

Like Prometheus fashioning the first human beings out of clay, the potters played with these metaphors, sometimes going even further, giving their pieces the precise anatomical shape of a breast (fig. 231), genitalia (for the foot of a cup in fig. 3), or a face, like the Dionysos and Silenus who make up a kantharos, a Dionysiac vase illustrating the ritual sequence of sacrifice, butchering, and banquet (figs. 4 and 5).

FIGS. 4 and 5. *Faces of Dionysos and Silenus make up a kantharos, a vase intended for the cult of the wine god.*

Other anatomical conceits turn the vase into a horn, a lobster-claw (fig. 6), or a hoof, associated with a pastoral scene (figs. 7 and 8). These are the extreme flights of fancy of artisans who more often produce simple, pure, and functional forms.

The names traditionally given to Greek vases are the legacy of 19th-century scholarship. These names are attested by ancient texts, but it is not always clear that the fifth-century Athenians used them to designate the same vases. It would be satisfying to clear up the matter, but in the absence of living testimony, this culture remains for us, to use M. I. Finley's apt phrase, "desperately foreign." Only the pictures themselves can help us to understand the function of the various vase shapes. They come to our aid by showing the vase and its use on the surface of the vase itself.

In this way, a hydria (fig. 9), intended to carry water from a fountain, is itself decorated with a scene of women carrying hydrias. In this case, the very name of the vase—from Greek *hydor*, "water"—indicates its function. Not all hydrias, however, present scenes like these. They may show other female activities (cf. fig. 124), sacrifices (cf. fig. 154), or hunting scenes (cf. fig. 95), to mention only themes to be discussed in this volume.

FIGS. 6, 7 and 8. *Other anatomical games turn the vase into a lobster-claw or a hoof.*

FIG. 9. *The public fountain-house* ▷ *where women carrying* hydrias *go to fetch water.*

FIG. 10. *An amphora bought from the potter would contain wine or oil.*

FIG. 11. *Careful decanting from the pelike to the alabastron so as not to lose a drop of the precious liquid.*

The picture, then, has only an arbitrary relationship to the vase. The amphora, a very common form, only rarely carries a picture of itself. Used for oil or wine, it is sometimes shown in commercial scenes. In figure 10, a man with purse in hand is buying an amphora, while on the pelike, a small squat amphora (fig. 11), the woman is buying the contents of the vase, as we can see from the funnel and alabastron held by the merchant. In general, however, vases of this type are decorated in a variety of ways. The large belly gives the painter room to execute many different types of scene, using both sides of the vase to present his subject (see fig. 155, a Panathenaic amphora, showing on one side the contest, on the other the presiding goddess of the festival), or painting two completely different scenes (cf. fig. 128, a bathing scene, and fig. 181, Dionysos among the vines).

The loutrophoros is a type of amphora with a particularly elongated shape. It is used to carry water for the bath that is a part of both marriage and funerary ritual, and it offers an extremely homogeneous iconography, composed almost exclusively of wedding or funeral scenes (figs. 12 and 144). In figure 12 the bridal procession, led by a flute-player, arrives at the gate of the house, which is guarded by a herm. Two women, one carrying a loutrophoros and the other, torches, form the procession, with the newlyweds following immediately behind.

The *lebes gamikos* (fig. 13), characterized by its double handles and elongated foot, is a woman's vase. A traditional wedding present, it appears in scenes of the gynaeceum and of wedding preparations.

FIG. 13. *A wedding present, the* lebes *is exchanged in the gynaeceum, the women's quarters.*

16

FIG. 12. *The woman carrying the loutrophoros precedes the newlyweds to the door of the house.*

Another category consists of various types of containers for perfume—the alabastron, aryballos, and lekythos. Figure 14 shows the funerary use of the lekythos. A woman standing beside a stele holds a basket with two lekythoi while a man adorns the tomb with ritual fillets. Such visits to the grave were occasions for offerings of cakes, wreathes, or perfume. As we can see by means of X-ray photography (fig. 15), funerary lekythoi often have a false bottom, so that only a small amount of perfume is needed to fill them.

These lekythoi, used in the cult of the dead, have their own distinctive technique—polychrome on a white ground—and their own specialized iconography. They form a class by themselves in Attic pottery and become numerous in the second half of the fifth century. Lekythoi in general are decorated according to the usual techniques and show a richly varied iconography. Thus, many of the themes we have chosen to discuss are illustrated by one or more lekythoi (cf. figs. 103, 123, 151, etc.). Such diversity undermines the hypothesis that this vase-type was used exclusively for funerary purposes. Designed to hold perfume or perfumed oil, lekythoi must have been among the toilet articles for women in the gynaeceum and for men in the gymnasium.

The vase category for which we have the most examples is that of the wine vessel. Often decorated with banquet scenes and Dionysiac images, these vases grant a central role to the god of wine, a more important role, certainly, than the one he occupies in the Greek pantheon.

The oinochoe, a sort of jug with a trilobate mouth, sometimes serves as a libation vase (fig. 16). Here, a maenad makes an offering of wine to a mask of Dionysos affixed to a column; foliage and rocks indicate the rural nature of the cult. Generally, however, the oinochoe is used during a banquet as the intermediate receptacle between large vases (krater, stamnos, dinos), where wine is mixed with water,

and the drinking vessels (skyphos, cup, kantharos). On a stamnos (fig. 17), two servants prepare the mixture. A large dinos on a stand receives the wine from two amphoras, while on each side an oinochoe resting on the ground is waiting to be filled and carried into the banquet room, which is shown on the other side of the vase (cf. fig. 174). As with the hydria, the name oinochoe, derived from *oinos* (wine), indicates its function.

The stamnos, even though decorated with varied images, is always represented as the principal vase of Dionysiac cult (cf. fig. 167). In figure 18, the idol of the god is absent, but one of his adepts fills a skyphos with a ladle, while a flute-player accompanies her with a song and another woman, skyphos in hand, helps herself to the sacred beverage. The cup is the drinking vessel *par excellence*. Flared in shape, it is held by the foot, as the drinker in figure 19 is doing. His neighbor twirls a cup on his fingertip, playing kottabos, a very popular game at the end of a banquet, which consists in tossing the dregs of wine at a previously selected target. The third banqueter plays the lyre and sings. A decorative frieze on the base of the bowl illustrates the most common types of drinking vessel: skyphos, kantharos, cup, and oinochoe. On

FIG. 17. *Dinos, amphora, oenochoe,* ▷ *all the vases needed to prepare the wine for a banquet.*

FIG. 18. *A mixture of wine and water fills the stamnos from which the women serve themselves in the rite of the wine-god Dionysos.*

19

FIGS. 19 and 20. *The joys of the banquet—music, games, and drink—decorate the cup, the drinking vessel par excellence.*

the other side (fig. 20), a flute-player accompanies the revels of the guests, while a serving-boy prepares to refill the cups.

The cup, however, is not used exclusively for banquets and wine drinking. In a cultic context, it becomes a libation vase (cf. fig. 33): at the door of a temple, a man pours wine over an altar. Like the oinochoe, the cup may be either a cult vessel or a drinking vessel.

We use this last example to emphasize the versatility of the vase shapes. Their domestic function adapts itself to the circumstances of daily or cultic life. Those examples we have shown, in which form is directly related to decoration, represent a minority of the thousands of scenes adorning Attic pottery. When we have established the corpus of images for a given theme, the diversity of shapes illustrating it shows that painters decorated their vases with great freedom and without regard to their function.

Thus there is no necessary correlation between the vases and the images—neither thematically, excepting specific series of vases used in marriage and funeral rites (cf. figs. 13, 14, 15), nor structurally, since the surface decorated by the painters does not necessarily follow the contours of the vase. In some instances, the shoulder of a hydria defines a surface distinct from the belly, and the two zones are decorated separately on different scales. In others, the hydria has a more rounded form and the picture extends from the shoulder to the belly in a double curvature which makes the subject at first difficult to interpret and poses formidable problems for the modern photographer (cf. figs. 10 and 14). The image is for the most part autonomous with respect to the vase. The shape defines the zones that the painter uses freely, framing and emphasizing his subject with decorative elements, or using all the available space around the vase, except for the handles.

Vases often have two sides (krater, amphora, stamnos), or two registers (krater, hydria), while cups offer three zones to be decorated (the interior tondo and the two exterior faces). There is very often no direct link, other than proximity, between the different images decorating a vase, and at times one of them seems simpler and more ordinary, thus giving a front and a back to the vase. Sometimes, however, the painter aims for a contrasting or complementary effect, arranging the various images in a sequence on the vase. The study of iconography must take these effects into account.

The versatility of vases in their domestic or cultic usage gives a characteristic, almost popular, quality to their imagery. The relation of the spectator to the image differs for a vase, a statue, or a temple. Ceramic iconography must be distinguished, not for its content, but for the way it is approached. The Athenian spectator does not move within a space populated by figures, but rather lives in the presence of circulating objects, of images that he holds in his hand and can associate with other images. The vase, carrier of images, is everywhere in the Greek city, especially in Athens, the principal producer of this art. A city of images: through this tremendously varied ceramic production, the city displays itself and stages its own fantasies.

For Further Reading

ON VASES IN GENERAL:

P. E. Arias and M. Hirmer, *Le vase grec.* Paris, 1962.
John Boardman, *Athenian Black Figure Vases.* London, 1974.
John Boardman, *Athenian Red Figure Vases.* London, 1975.
R. M. Cook, *Greek Painted Pottery.* London, 1960.
I. Scheibler, *Griechische Töpferkunst.* Munich, 1983.
F. Villard, *Les vases grecs.* Paris, 1956.

VASE SHAPES:

W. Froehner, *Anatomie des vases antiques.* Paris, 1876.
H. Gericke, *Gefässdarstellungen auf griechischen Vasen.* Berlin, 1970.
G. Richter and M. J. Milne, *Shapes and Names of Athenian Vases.* New York, 1935.

TECHNIQUE:

J. V. Noble, *The Techniques of Painted Attic Pottery.* New York, 1965.

CHAPTER II

Entering the Imagery

CLAUDE BÉRARD AND
JEAN-LOUIS DURAND

Shifty Images

Reading an ancient image demands of the modern observer a kind of mental gymnastics which is not complicated, but which requires gradual training. We must always keep in mind that we are cut off from the conditions that prevailed at its creation. Neither texts, whether literary or epigraphic, nor excavations, nor the extant body of imagery allow a complete reconstruction of the historical moment which would make the document in question comprehensible. In the best of cases, the archaeologist uncovers a piece of information in one place, a point of comparison in another, and many of these pieced together are needed to master the situation. To illustrate the process of deciphering an image, we have chosen a classical wine krater (fig. 21a) whose style is close to that of one of the great known masters, Polygnotos. Put simply, this krater now in Ferrara was created in the time of Perikles, Phidias, and the Parthenon. The frieze that runs continuously around the belly of the vase has never received a complete and definitive commentary. One reason for the lack of success is the commentators' insistance on naming the different actors in the scene that unfolds before us, even though the protagonists' exact identity is not necessarily the key to a more profound understanding of the image, and may even conceal its richness.

FIG. 21a. *The cult images in their sanctuary.*

FIG. 21b. *The arrival of the priestesses with sacred flutes and veiled basket.*

As we begin this reading, it is important to note that the frieze is continuous. There is no break in continuity, even under the handles. We can see, however, that the painter has organized his composition so as to make the best possible use of the surfaces put at his disposition by the potter. There is a principal side (A) with figures larger than the others on the vase, which includes architectural elements, and a secondary side (B) which shows only groups of dancers (figs. 21c-e). A first trip around the vase enables us to establish an order of reading: the eye focuses first on the central group of side A, which looks right, towards a procession coming from the left. What we see, therefore, is a meeting between a static, seated group and a dynamic, standing group. The flute-player located at the left of the picture (fig. 21a) confirms this order of reading: he turns his back to the seated group.

23

FIG. 22. *A sculptural group on the Acropolis: divine forces in action.*

The rest of the frieze (B) is made up of several groups of dancers who face each other and appear to whirl about, taking no notice of the processional movement leading to the central group. As proof of this I note that the female flute-player integrated among the dancers faces the male flute-player (figs. 21e, f). One would thus interpret this scene as a turbulent choreography that encircles the representation just as the entire frieze surrounds the vase and its contents, the wine. After this preliminary, and superficial, attempt, we proceed to a more precise angle of attack, examining the obvious difference in size between the seated central group and the other actors. This disproportion gives rise to several observations. We note, for example, that not only is the seated couple larger than life (according to the scale set by the other participants), but also that they are enthroned on a sort of pedestal while the feet of the other figures crowd the lower decorative border of the picture. This larger couple is framed by columns. The man is bearded and his head is ringed by snakes like some of the dancers, while the woman is crowned with a diadem. They are in similar hieratic postures and each holds a scepter in one hand and a libation cup in the other. Finally, there is a small lion posed very artificially on the woman's left arm. And that is not all. This group cannot be separated from the right-hand section of the frieze. In fact, the libation cups are not merely decorative accessories or attributes; they are functional: liquid flows and spreads to the foot of the altar in front of the pedestal. (This essential detail is scarcely visible in the photograph, since it is painted in added white, which is extremely fugitive.) Although static, this mysterious couple thus participates in the general action, carrying out a libation, as if in response to the musicians and dancers who frame them.

We are in the presence of a complex combination of figurative elements. By analyzing the rules that structure this composition we may gradually arrive at the meaning of the scene. It is worth stressing that, for these rules to be defined and put to use, it is necessary to consider this document in the context of a series of images, comparing the different combinations that shape these new images. An isolated image will most likely remain mute; a network of images, on the other hand, begins to give up its meanings through the similarities and differences shown by the combinations. Here is the major difficulty of interpretation: in order to measure the variations from image to image and to establish the rules of composition followed by the artisans, one must keep in mind the whole body of imagery simultaneously. This mental acrobatics remains the best way to approach the ancient conditions of creation.

Let us illustrate these theoretical remarks with several examples. On a krater in Berlin (fig. 22), we see again one of the elements described above, the pedestal, supporting a group of very familiar figures, Achilles and Ajax playing dice. At the center of the image, behind the gaming table, stands the silhouette of the goddess Athena in profile looking left towards a small winged Victory, which runs along her right arm to crown the victor. On the far left, a figure makes a gesture of surprise and astonishment. Here again we notice the same discrepancy seen on the Ferrara krater (fig. 21): the feet of the astonished spectator, on the left, are placed directly on the line that frames the scene while the two epic warriors crouch on the pedestal. To this purely formal difference corresponds a difference of existential status, as it were. The spectator with his feet on the ground is an ordinary Athenian citizen, while the two figures on the pedestal are heroes. The pedestal thus serves as a base for figures who belong unmistakably to the legendary mythic-heroic cycle of the Trojan war. The ensemble portrays a group of *sculptures*. The artist has moreover added a third register, that of religion. In fact, the goddess Athena is also represented according to a sculptural type, precisely that of the statue installed by Phidias in the Parthenon. There also, a Victory was posed in the hand of the goddess. On the krater in Berlin (fig. 22), however, the Victory is animated, incarnating

25

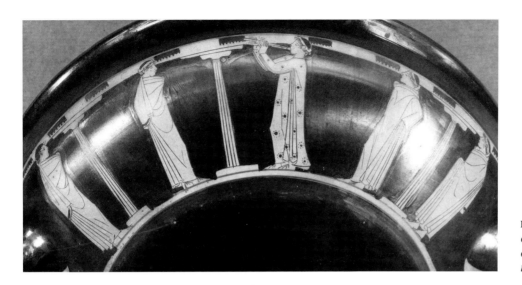

FIG. 23. *The wooden Doric columns of a stoa serve as a frame to a chorus of men (flute and theatrical spectacle).*

the divine energies which miraculously intervene in the action and provoke the amazement of the Athenian. Although the statue of Athena identifies the setting as the sanctuary of the Acropolis, the pedestal in this context is an element whose function is entirely secular. On the other hand, in the first krater examined (fig. 21), the value of the same element is charged with a sacred connotation by its relation to the columns of the altar. At the same time it denotes the sculptural character of the seated couple and indicates that they are statues of gods. The liquid flows from their sacred cups according to the same principle as that which animates the Victory on the arm of Athena. The source of the action—a mystical element in the religious vision transmitted by the painter—resides in the symbolic efficacy of the rites of music and dance practiced before the temple. This is the meaning of the setting composed of the combined elements of cult statues, columns, and altar. In this way we can explain the difference in scale between the cult images on their base and in their temple, on the one hand, and the priests, the priestesses, and the faithful on the other.

We may stress once more that it is always the combination of elements that is significant in each case. The columns, for example, may refer to many different types of structure. Only the context will enable us to distinguish a house, propylaion, stoa, theater, gymnasium, etc. The colonnade that we see on a cup in New York (fig. 23) may be part of any kind of portico. The presence of flute-players and young singers, and the Doric columns (whose bases show them to be wooden), suggests a stoa or a theater scene rather than a temple. In the same way, the male flute-player on the krater in Ferrara (fig. 21f) could be described as a priest, since we have established that the locus of the action is a sanctuary; but this same flute-player may be repeated in completely everyday, secular scenes, of the gymnasium, for example (fig. 24). The same is true for the female flute-player who plays her instrument before the altar on the right-hand side of the Ferrara krater (fig. 21b). Here she can be identified as a priestess; the function of her music is in fact defined by the sacral context of the frieze. But in a banquet scene on a krater in the Louvre (fig. 25), which shows a group of men sprawled on couches during a joyful drinking bout, the young woman who plays the flute has no right to the title of priestess. She is not necessarily a slave or courtesan, but perhaps a professional musician hired for the evening.

The constituent elements of the image are thus stable and constant. These

make up the repertoire of minimal formal units, which is common to all artisans and familiar to all clients. The combinations, however, vary, and it is in these combinations that we find the meaning of a picture. In order to progress in our understanding of the frieze on the Ferrara krater (fig. 21), we must examine every element of the image. We have not yet spoken of the priestess who leads the procession while holding a veiled object on her head. Although veiled, the characteristic shape of the object, pointed on one side, higher on the other, makes it easily identifiable as a kind of basket, the winnowing fan (in Greek, *liknon*), which one often sees unveiled in marriage processions (figs. 26, 135). The winnowing fan is in origin an agricultural implement used to clean the grains of wheat. This purificatory function quickly conferred on it a religious, and then a symbolic, connotation. It is used in certain ceremonies connected with the goddess of cereals, Demeter, but one encounters it frequently also in the Dionysiac cycle (cf. fig. 209).

It can also be used in other contexts, for example as a cradle. The context supplies its meaning. That it is covered with a veil shows that it is filled with ritual and sacred objects which may not be seen by random passersby. The procession is just

FIG. 24. *Musical gymnastics to the rhythm of the flute.*

FIG. 25. *Drinking to the sound of the flute.*

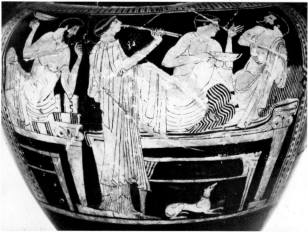

arriving, but one may conjecture that later the mysterious contents of the basket will be revealed. The contrast of the exposed winnowing fan in marriage processions (fig. 26) to the covered one in our ceremony thus allows us to specify their respective functions.

We will conclude this commentary with an examination of the groups of dancers. It is extremely unusual in Greek imagery of this date to see groups composed on one side of adults and adolescents, even children (figs. 21c, d, e), and on the other side, of dancers of both sexes. There is in fact a young boy who is using a kind of castanets (I do not believe, as some have maintained, that they are *krotales*, bones that are elongated, not rounded, in shape), his head crowned by snakes, facing a young woman who is collapsing, bewitched by the rhythm (figs. 21d, e). It also seems to me that one can identify a young man on the left-hand side of face B (fig. 21c), despite the similarity of his cassock with the costume of his feminine counterpart. His tunic is short, like that of the child just described, while none of the women is shown in a short dress; his coiffure, moreover, is masculine. Such observations show the difficulties of analysis: up to this point we have dealt with no scene comparable to this one. Dionysiac groups, for example, are composed mainly of female dancers (cf. chaps. 8 and 9), and men only participate in them in the guise of satyrs, which transforms their existential status (figs. 196ff). This is not the case here. The attitudes of the dancers, however, show great similarities to Dionysiac choreography, the same contortions of the body, the same jerking of the limbs (cf. fig. 202), the same use of music. The music has as its base percussion instruments—great bronze drums resounding hollowly and little castanets with their dry clicking, whose rhythm is underlined by the strident sounds of the flutes. The Dionysiac maenad of figure 27 offers a perfect parallel to the female dancers on the frieze of the Ferrara krater (fig. 21c, d). She also strikes a tympanon, her hair falls in long curls over her shoulders, and snakes hiss about her head. Facing her, playing the flute, we find, however, not a priest in a sumptuous embroidered costume, but a naked satyr. Dionysos holding a thyrsos is in the center of the composition. On the Ferrara krater frieze, no thyrsos, no crown of ivy, no vase of Dionysiac shape allows us to push the interpretation into the realm of the god of wine. At the most, one could say that the atmosphere is somewhat similar: orgiastic, ecstatic dance, spellbinding music, manipulation of snakes. But the differences are too profound to force the parallel. As for the snakes, they appear on the heads of other figures, such as the hellish Furies who menace Orestes the matricide, when he has taken refuge at the omphalos, sacred stone of Apollo and center of the Delphic sanctuary (fig. 28). This last image confers a chthonic, underworld connotation on the snakes, which, we may recall, also surround the head of the bearded god enthroned at the center of face A of the krater in Ferrara (fig. 21a).

Have we made any progress? We may have frustrated the reader, who will demand the names of the actors, or at least the protagonists. We have not given them, both out of intellectual honesty and because they do not seem indispensable to an understanding of the image. Certainly, the divine couple could be a chthonic Dionysos flanked by an underworld Persephone, honored by Hipta, the mystic priestess who carries the mysterious winnowing fan; but they could equally well be Sabazios and Kybele or another couple, known but rarely celebrated in the secret rites of a sect. Nothing permits us to decide for sure and we are thus reduced to a guessing-game.

It has been important to us nonetheless to comment on this document that comes out of pure classicism, to call to mind that Greek society is also a society in uproar, as Roger Caillois has said, and that, behind the façade of the Greek miracle, obscure but well-rooted forces continue to disturb the hearts of the faithful. It was also our aim to show how, in approaching a picture, it is necessary to enter the imagery, even if the analysis of the system, in the absence of documents, yields inconclusive results. Such experience can only be useful.

Spatial Variations

The space of the artists is constructed to the measure of the human being. Landscape and still-life are almost unknown. As Rainer Maria Rilke had already observed in 1902 (*Von der Landschaft*), not only the architecture of the city, but even the seas, plains, and mountains did not yet exist as a frame for human activities. A tondo on a cup in Boston (fig. 29) shows, however, that this lack of interest in the natural surroundings is not the result of a fundamental incapacity to draw what is picturesque in an admittedly ordinary scene. The young man fishing crouched on a cliff of the shore shows a sensibility which will find expression above all in the Hellenistic period. A lobster-trap rests on the sea floor and various curious fish indicate that the fisherman will not return home empty-handed. Skulking in an anderground cavity, an octopus lies in wait for his own prey, or perhaps bides his time until calm is restored.

FIG. 29. *Seascape: the little fisherman.*

FIG. 30. *Mountain scene: the Bacchic cave.*

In many examples, large wavy sections suggest rocky hills and especially the caves that shelter Dionysiac rites (fig. 30). Even today in the pine forests that dominate Athens, one finds Dionysiac sanctuaries where the cave adorned with ivy, the spring, and the giant plane trees served as a setting for the revels of the thiasos. Elsewhere wild vines still climb trunks and bunches of grapes balance high above the ground, striking images of the cult of Dionysos of the Tree (*Dendrites*), well-attested by the texts.

These two images are exceptional in that no functional stone construction disturbs the purity of nature. On the tondo of a cup in the Villa Giulia (fig. 31), however, an altar is sheltered under the vault of a cavern. Here *homo faber* has intervened. Nature is exploited in the service of the multiple relations that human beings undertake with the gods.

The place *par excellence* of the altar is not, however, in the open spaces, but in the city. The city is filled with them, whether in the community's religious space,

FIG. 31. *A sacrificial altar outside the city.*

FIG. 32. *A sacrificial altar within the city.*

the sanctuaries (cf. chap. 7), in public places such as the agora, theater, gymnasium, or in private ones, such as the courtyard of a house.

The altar, in front of which a young woman carries out a ritual act (fig. 32), holding a sacrificial basket whose contents are decorated with branches, indicates more the value of the religious act than the place; the space remains indeterminate. On the other hand, the column that accompanies the altar on a cup in Tarquinia (fig. 33) aids in reading the image. A man performs a libation accompanied by a gesture of reverence towards the divinity. Does the combination of column and altar indicate a sanctuary or a private house? Is the column the first of a colonnade marking the entrance to the temple (cf. fig. 154), or does it support the vestibule of the house (cf. fig. 140), thus locating the rite in a private space? It is for the images to answer.

The kiss exchanged by the two partners in an intimate scene (fig. 34) would be difficult to locate in the sacred setting of a sanctuary. Indeed, the painter has even substituted a chair for the altar. The column denotes private space. The possibilities for combinations are numerous and the richness of the repertoire multiplies the solutions. On a cup in the Louvre (fig. 35), a door replaces the column, but is it the door of a temple, or the door of a house? Here we see the door of a house from the outside, the side of the street and the altar, if we may venture a guess based on an interior scene on another cup in the Louvre (fig. 36), where the scene is sketched from the side of the room, as we see from the large hand-mirror in the background and a stool substituted for the altar. But on a cup in the Villa Giulia (fig. 37), it is the column and not the door that combines with the stool. In place of the altar on the cup in Tarquinia (fig. 33) a stool is substituted in figure 36. Does this mean that the stool is placed outside? The image on a cup in Naples (fig. 38) gives us an affirmative answer, since the altar cannot be located inside the house. Moreover, above the   31

FIG. 33. *A sacrificial altar in front of a temple or a house (meaning of the column)?*

FIG. 34. *The kiss in front of the house (column and chair).*

FIG. 35. *The altar before the door of the house.*

FIG. 36. *Interior of the house (note position of the mirror).*

seat, the gymnast's gear (sponge, strigil, and flacon of perfumed oil) recalls the exterior space of the exercise tracks (cf. fig. 126) just as the mirror in figure 36 refers to the interior space of the women's private apartments (cf. fig. 138).

Finally, on a cup in the Louvre (fig. 39), is the couple shown beside the door inside or outside? If outside, they are leaving the house (but there is no altar); if inside, they enter a room (but there is no bed). The economy of signs is such that the image remains ambiguous. Only the examination of a richer corpus of images would allow us to specify the moment of action. For example, the series of marriage processions presented in chapter 6, "The Order of Women," especially figure 139c, encourages us to see here the newlyweds' first moments of intimacy.

The opposition between outside and inside is sometimes expressed more explicitly. The potter and seller of vases is seated in his shop (fig. 40), while the woman drawing water works outside, in the open air (fig. 41).

The athletic gear that we have observed in figure 38 takes us to the tracks of the gymnasium (cf. fig. 126). It is in fact at the gymnasium that we see a young man with a javelin depicted on a cup in Boston (fig. 42). The basin filled with water for washing could be part of the furnishings of a private space (cf. fig. 141), but its combina-

FIG. 37. *The house seen from the courtyard.*

FIG. 38. *The altar of the gymnasium (note the athlete's kit).*

tion with the stadium-marker can only refer to the public space of the official gymnasium. The marker may give way to one of the herms frequently set up in gymnasia (fig. 43). The location of the scene remains clear, even when the basin is replaced by an altar (fig. 44). The grouping of figures 38, 42, 43, and 44 thus completes the construction of the gymnastic space: the equipment for cleansing the naked athlete's body, the basin for the water, the stadium marker, the seat reserved for the trainer or judge, the altar for sacrifice, the pillar of Hermes, the presiding god, whose aggressively jutting phallus brings luck to the contestant who invokes him.

This game of signs may seem difficult to decipher, but only at first glance. Contact with these images tends to create a familiarity with the system, which allows one to move with relative ease in this pictorial world. The examples we have given show that figurative elements combine in an almost mechanical fashion to produce a meaning as devoid of ambiguity as possible. From this perspective, the relation of reference to reality is less important than the relation of meaning. The artist constructs his image with reference to other images rather than by faithfully conforming to the laws of an almost photographic reproduction of daily life.

C. B.

FIG. 41. *The courtyard of a house: fetching water.*

FIG. 43. *The gymnasium (basin and herm).*

FIG. 42. *The gymnasium (marker and basin).*

For Further Reading

C. Bérard, *Anodoi.* Essai sur l'imagerie des passages chthoniens. Bibliotheca Helvetica Romana 13, 1974.
C. Bérard, *Espace de la cité grecque—espace des imagiers. Degrés* (Brussels) 35-36, 1983, C.
Essais sémiotiques, ed. C. Bérard. *Etudes de Lettres* (Lausanne) 1983, fasc. 4.

FIG. 44. *The gymnasium (herm and altar).*

FIG. 45. *A young man carrying a leg of mutton—where is he coming from and where is he going?*

Variations of Gesture

Images can only be constituted by putting together graphic elements juxtaposed in a kind of collage: objects, constructions such as an altar or column, vegetation such as branches or fronds, living creatures, human or animal. Men's gestures and postures tie these elements together, thus organizing the image spatially. This is so much the case that the gesture itself can become the object of the composition: it is sufficient to stand for the ensemble from which it has been removed and into which it must be reinserted in order for it to be understood.

On an amphora in Boston (fig. 45), a young man wrapped in a voluminous robe advances towards the right, carrying a freshly boned leg of mutton. His crown indicates a festival; the leg of mutton is a reference to sacrifice. But the gesture captured in the image is fixed in a particular moment and, for a contemporary, it must have been interpretable. The spectator must have been able to reinsert it in the program of gestures from which it was taken. The young man is coming from an unspecified point in space toward which he looks back; he is heading towards another point where he will do something with the leg of mutton he carries. This is impossible to understand without knowing the entire repertoire of gestures, specific to that civilization; there is a vast system of possible combinations that covers each instant of daily life.

Greek gods on vases have human form, and thus cannot avoid gesture. They in their turn are included in the array of gestural programs characteristic of the Greek world. Thus Eros, a winged youth, on a lekythos in Palermo (fig. 46), advances carrying a piece of boned meat. Like the ephebe in Boston, he is caught in transit, indicating with head and hand the point of departure, in a context left entirely to the imagination. In the complete visual program to which the carrying of the leg of mutton belongs, the power of Eros can manifest itself and be invested in young people. There is no other way for the image to tell of mythical beings than to show them assuming the gestures of the men among whom they move. One could of course show Eros flying, but the carrying of the mutton indicates the god's power

36

FIG. 46. *Eros carrying a leg of mutton: a mythic figure in the gestural space of human beings.*

For Further Reading

G. Neumann, *Gesten und Gebärden in der griechischen Kunst.* Berlin, 1965.

over the young men who also appear as carriers of this cut of meat, by placing him in the same context in which they themselves are likely to act.

Reality, everyday life, implies the intervention of the gods. Their relationships are indicated, once again, by gesture. Even in trying to set himself apart, a god cannot escape human gestures.

Thus the images are based on choices from the continuum of gestures that inform social existence. These choices present the moments and situations in which, in the eyes of contemporary Greeks, the values of their own society are most clearly seen and expressed.

J.-L. D.

FIG. 47. *A handsome athlete performing his toilette in front of a basin.*

FIG. 49. *Jumpin*

FIG. 48. *A winning athlete crowned by two Victories.*

CHAPTER III

The World of the Warrior

FRANÇOIS LISSARRAGUE

FIG. 50. *A javelin toss.*

FIG. 51. *A discus throw.*

The youth, in the imagery of red figure, is often shown as an athlete. Tirelessly replicated, his image incessantly repeats the beauty of the human body. On a pelike in Berlin (fig. 47), a young crowned athlete washes himself beside a large basin. He holds a bronze scraper, the strigil, with which he cleans his body. Above the basin hang two accessories: the kit containing a sponge and a vial of perfume, and a sandal. At the center of the picture, on the stone basin, is an emblematic inscription—*kalos*, beautiful. All this, in effect, plays on the idea of the beautiful. The arrested moment of the toilette permits the display of the young man's slender body, surrounded by the accessories of this activity. The image depicts beauty and speaks of it, abstractly, with an inscription placed on the basin, defining it as the very font of beauty. It is in short the word itself that is displayed here.

Athletic exercise is above all a chance for the artist to show youthful beauty, the gift of the gods. But this exercise is also directed toward that essential driving force in Greek life, the *agon*, contest, rivalry among the young, and the quest for victory. To win at the games, in Athens as at Olympia or elsewhere, is to win divine glory. To the first gift of the gods, beauty, is added a second, victory. Hence the development, within the imagery, of allegorical representations of Nike crowning the victor. On a cup in the Louvre (fig. 48), the altar and the boundary-marker establish the link between religious and agonistic space, and we see once again the word *kalos*, beautiful, which makes the meaning of the picture explicit. This word *KALOS* repeatedly invades the images on pottery produced from approximately 510 to 480—as if it were not enough for painters to show youths preparing, leaping, stretching muscles and limbs—to the point of filling the entire field of the tondi ornamenting the cups. The word often comes to take over the representation which is less concerned with the technical character of the exercises and more with the physical beauty that they display. Characteristic exercises are jumping (fig. 49), javelin-throwing (figs. 50 and 51), wrestling (fig. 52), armed running (fig. 53) and dancing (fig. 54). The great variety of exercices is a preparation as much for the harmonious development of the body as for strictly military activities.

Thus a cup in Berlin (fig. 53) shows an armed runner leaping smartly. His shield is decorated with the silhouette of a runner like himself, in an infinite regress which

39

FIG. 52. *Wrestling.*

FIG. 53. *An armed runner.*

FIG. 54. *An armed dancer.*

underlines the importance of this exercise and which produces the effect of movement by the play of concentric circles of the tondo and the shields. On a cup in the Louvre (fig. 54), we see another type of athletic military exercise, the armed dance or *pyrrhike*, lead by a flute-player (cf. fig. 125).

Certain images allow one a glimpse of practices somewhere between athletic exercise, marginalized forms of war, and ritual behavior. Three vases belonging to the same series permit us to grasp the whole. On the example from the Louvre (fig. 55) three young ephebes are crouching, carrying small light shields decorated with an apotropaic eye, wearing Scythian caps rather than helmets. They carry no weapons and seem to be miming an ambush. Their equipment is radically different from that of the hoplites. Their headgear and shields are "barbarian" in type and they have neither the breastplate nor the greaves of the Greek foot soldier. On a vase in Pontecagnano (fig. 56), the warriors, here again crouching, almost crawling, are well equipped with helmets and round shields, but they are nude like athletes, and armed with stones and swords, hardly typical hoplite weapons. Lastly, on an-

FIG. 55. *Light-armed youths in an ambush.*

FIG. 56. *Combat with sword and stone.*

FIG. 57. *Mimed ambush around an altar.*

FIG. 60. *Armed owl: epiphany of Athena or metamorphosis of the warrior?*

FIG. 58. *Ambush: between hunting and war.*

other vase, in Heidelberg (fig. 57), we find the same "Scythian" ephebes, crouching and unarmed, around an altar behind which there rises a palm tree, perhaps the indication of a connection with Artemis, with whom this tree is associated and who presides over the passage from youth to adult warrior.

Ambush, trickery, and hunting are marginal practices with respect to hoplite warfare, waged in broad daylight in the open on flat ground. The hoplites advance, locked together in closed ranks. Youths, on the other hand, lie in wait, crouched hidden behind bushes as on a cup in Cambridge (fig. 58). The plants are not merely landscaping; they play an essential role, indicating not so much a place as a kind of warfare. The two groups of warriors are distinct. Some, with raised helmets and round shields and armed with lances, have no breastplates; the others wear boots and broad-brimmed hats and carry two lances. This is the traditional equipment of the hunter.

Here we find ourselves in the space between hunting and war. The inverse of this relationship is seen on a cup in the Louvre (fig. 59) on which deer are pursued by four hunters, of whom one is helmeted and another has a shield and greaves. The rarity of these images, liminal in bringing together hunting and hoplite war, which usually inhabit separate spheres, allows us to grasp the essential opposition between these activities that the city organizes but keeps distinct.

The world of the young, the athletes who prepare themselves to become citizen warriors, is precisely the place where these categories can still intermingle before being put definitively in their place. In Athens, to be a citizen is to take one's place in the ranks to defend the ancestral land. Athena, the patron goddess of the city, is the warrior *par excellence*, and the equivalence is so strong that a painter can, 43

FIG. 59. *Hunters armed as foot soldiers.*

FIG. 61. *Libation and leave-taking on the departure of a warrior.*

without ambiguity, arm the owl, the goddess's emblematic animal, to produce an extraordinary epiphany of Athena, a synthetic image of the divine bird, the armed goddess, and the citizen-soldier (fig. 60).

Centering on the hoplite, the artists developed a number of images that emphasize the individual role of the warrior in relation to other classes in the city rather than his collective activity on the field of battle. Scenes showing the phalanx, the compact group of hoplites, are quite rare. The artists prefer a duel of heroes to the anonymous combat of masses of warriors.

Above all, however, images are most frequently constructed around the various rituals that organize the relationship between the warrior and the members of the family group, women or old men. Thus one may find various scenes marking the departure of the warrior—arming, offerings, divination—or the return of the hero.

44

In all these series, the image proceeds by the juxtaposition of figures, according to a fairly simple iconographic code. Aside from the hoplite, recognizable by his arms, one may find the archer, a marginal fighter, a mere assistant who never takes an active part in the rituals of departure or return. Among those who have no part in war, who remain in the city, the image presents the woman, whose place is central, and the bearded old man, once a hoplite, but now the repository of political authority. Here again there is no decoration, but the simple confrontation of those who, brought together in this way, make up the essential categories of Greek society in the eyes of those who set the scene.

Reduced to the barest minimum, the departure scene figured on a stamnos in London (fig. 61) conveys the essential information. In the center, an armed hoplite grasps the hand of a bearded figure in a gesture of farewell filled with gravity. The handshake, less common in ancient Greece than in our times, keeps all its symbolic force as a bond physically uniting two beings. The two men look at one another, the embodiment of two age classes who meet to hand down from one to the other the role of making war. On the right, a woman holds a pitcher and a shallow bowl, ritual instruments for the libation, almost obligatory for marking a departure or

FIG. 62. *Libation and taking-up of weapons for the young hunter.*

return. The woman pours wine into the bowl, a part of which will be poured on the ground for the gods, while the rest will be drunk by each of the participants in turn. The performance of this libation, which combines offering and sharing, marks the bonds linking each member of the group to the others and affirms the relationship that unites this group with the gods. It is usually the woman who carries the equipment necessary to this operation, assuming, then, an essential role in the center of the family group. Through her, the permanence of the group is guaranteed by ritual means.

In the same way, the woman occupies an important place in scenes of arming, since she carries the armor with which the hoplite equips himself, thus turning the man into a warrior. Women provide the city-state with soldiers. The imagery shows them present at the very moment of departure, indicating this essential function. A

45

krater from Tübingen (fig. 62) juxtaposes these two moments: libation on the left, arming on the right of the tableau. Several elements of this picture allow us to infer a double transition. First of all, the religious and ritual character of the libation is indicated by the presence of the altar, perhaps of Apollo or Artemis, if the palm is to be taken as a reference to the divinities of Delos. Thus we have a transition from the domestic space to that of war. What is more, the warrior preparing to leave is shown here in a short cloak, with a broad-brimmed hat, armed with two lances, just like the hunters on the cup in Cambridge (fig. 58). Depicted as a hunter, he receives the arms of a hoplite. Thus we see the change of status, a kind of investiture of the future hoplite.

Behind these arming scenes which highlight the individual figure of the isolated warrior, we find traces of various mythic models which turn the warrior into an epic hero. On an amphora in Munich (fig. 63), the inscriptions lead us to identify Hector, in the center, between his aged father Priam and his mother Hecuba. One notices the passive role of the father in contrast to the active role of the mother, which corresponds to the earlier formula of the mother as progenitor of the hero.

This woman presenting the arms, an anonymous or mythic mother, a Hecuba or a Thetis, is often the object of another transposition in the imagery. For her the painters substitute a helmeted, armed woman who is none other than Athena, the civic goddess, presiding over the arming of the citizen-soldier (fig. 64). In this way we see the paradox which makes every citizen-hoplite in some way a child of Athena.

On an amphora in Würzburg (fig. 65), the goddess remains at the side of the hoplite, whom she accompanies as his double, under the eyes of Hermes, god of passage, and an unidentified woman. From the human to the divine, the hoplite, the companion of Athena, is elevated to the level of the heroes of epic, at whose sides the gods do not hesitate to engage in battle.

Finally, just as with the athlete, the ideology of victory leads the image-makers to produce scenes in which Victory herself intervenes, either to restore to the warrior his weapons or to offer a libation, as on a krater in Ferrara (fig. 66), where the

FIG. 63. *Hector arming himself, flanked by his parents, Priam and Hecuba.*

FIG. 64. *The arming of a hoplite* ▷ *under the eye of Athena.*

FIG. 65. *The departure of the warrior with Athena by his side.*

46

FIG. 66. *Departure: a woman carries* ▷ *the armor, while Nike performs the libation.*

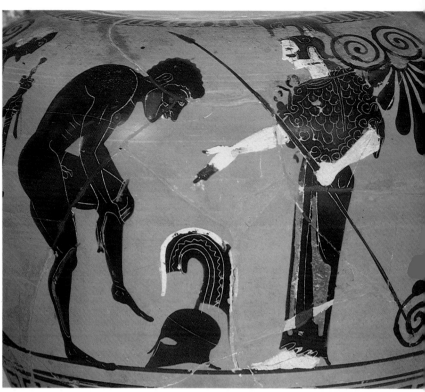

transition is indicated by a column which articulates the interior and exterior space, the human and the divine realms.

In this way the image constitutes a discourse on the place of the warrior in society, with respect to the family and the gods. On another level, through the death of the warrior, the relation between this world and the next is depicted by a visual conceit, as on a vase in Cambridge (fig. 67), which consists in constructing an arming-scene around a funeral stele. The warrior is no longer standing in an abstract domestic space, but sitting on the steps of his own tomb, receiving from a woman the arms of the combat in which he has met a glorious hero's death.

Among the many departure scenes, a small number shows the precise moment in which the entrails of the sacrificial victim are examined to obtain a response about the future. Always organized around the same central group, these illustrations show different intervening figures, who, by their juxtaposition, construct an image of the social body. On an amphora in Würzburg (fig. 68), a young naked slave, at the center of the picture, carries a bundle of viscera to be submitted to examination—hieroscopy. The active role is played by the hoplite himself, already armed. The divinatory operation, an examination of the entrails of the

FIG. 67. *Arming, at the tomb of the warrior.*

FIG. 68. *Divination: a hoplite examines the liver presented by a young slave.*

FIG. 69. *Ajax carrying the body of Achilles.*

FIG. 70. *A warrior carrying his dead companion.*

49

FIG. 71. *The return of the dead man, between the woman and the warrior.*

sacrificial victim, does not consist in asking the gods about the future, but more precisely about the appropriateness of the moment chosen. The question is not "What is to be done?" or "What will come of it?" but "Is this the right time?" asked only at the moment of departure. If the entrails, particularly the liver, look as they should, this is interpreted as a favorable response.

We see that it is the warrior who carries out this examination, while the other figures, mere spectators, only participate with a gesture. Often, in this series, behind the slave carrying the liver, there is an old man who raises his hand as if to comment on the sacred message. The woman, when present, is relegated to the background, the margins of the image. While she plays a role in the arming, she apparently does not participate in the decision or in the action itself.

Working from this series of images, which reveals a precise combination of elements rather than the mere repetition of a given model, we can identify the rigorously defined positions and roles that are repeated in the series of the return of the dead warrior.

The painters present death in battle through the epic tradition of the "beautiful death." The hero who lies dead on the ground is in no way horrible or repulsive; on the contrary, his body is lovely to look at, and his hair magnificent. Thus Homer describes Hector, just killed by Achilles: "He spoke and stripped from the corpse his bronze pike, which he left by his side; then he took the bloody armor from his shoulders. The sons of the Achaeans ran up from all sides. They marveled at the stature and the admirable beauty of Hector."

Just as the function of epic is to sing the exploits of heroes, and no heroism is possible without a poet to perpetuate the memory, so here, the image plays a commemorative role in making the dead man an epic hero. When an inscription explicitly gives him a name, it is most often Achilles (fig. 69). Most of the images, however, are anonymous. The scene has nothing to do with the official funerals reserved for the war-dead as we know them from the speeches pronounced on the occasion. The painters do not represent the civic ceremony, but rather, as on an amphora in Munich (fig. 70), the transport of a warrior with richly adorned armor, in transition from the battlefield to the domestic and urban space where he will be received and mourned by his people. The woman and the old man frequently take their place around the dead man (fig. 71), just as around the warrior arming. From corpse to hero, this is the transition that the imagery shows us, playing, in its own fashion, the role of the epic memory.

From departure to return, the social group organizes itself around the warrior, the central figure, as the evidence shows. When all figures are absent, and the image is, as it were, emptied out, there remains, as on this vase from the Louvre (fig. 72), nothing but the armor of the warrior. This is not a still life—a genre unknown to Attic painters—but a picture reduced to its essentials. The panoply thus isolated is enough to indicate, almost abstractly, all the values of war and heroism of which Attic imagery provides innumerable examples.

FIG. 72. *Panoply: the implicit presence of the warrior or hero.*

For Further Reading

ON SPORTS:

E. N. Gardiner, *Athletics of the Ancient World.* Oxford, 1930.
J. Jüthner, *Die athletische Leibesübungen der Griechen.* 2 vols. Vienna, 1965-69.
R. Patrucco, *Lo sport nella Grecia antica.* Florence, 1972.

ON THE WARRIOR:

P. Ducrey, *Guerre et guerriers dans la Grèce antique.* Paris, 1985.
J.-L. Durand and F. Lissarrague, "Les entrailles de la cité" *Hephaistos* 1, 1979, 92-108.
F. Lissarrague, *L'Autre guerrier; archers, peltastes et cavaliers dans l'imagerie attique.* Paris-Rome (forthcoming 1988).
W. Wrede, "Kriegers Ausfahrt." *Ath. Mitt.* 41, 1916, 216ff.

FIG. 73. Procession.

CHAPTER IV

Sacrificial Slaughter and Initiatory Hunt

JEAN-LOUIS DURAND AND

ALAIN SCHNAPP

Man stands between beasts and gods, but this relationship cannot be expressed in just any way. First and foremost, the flesh of beasts serves as food for men.

To eat whatever comes to hand means to eat like beasts. Rules are needed, to avoid the risk of becoming bestial, of transforming oneself into an animal. Thus partaking of meat becomes a religious act. And the whole complex of rules that allows men to eat animals under the eyes of the gods, is organized into a system that we call, for lack of a better term, sacrifice, in which everyone has a defined place and role. First, those to be eaten must be neither too close, nor too remote, domesticated but no more than that. Men, meanwhile, offer the gods the smoke of burning altars on which the spitted entrails crackle in the flame. To eat this meat, to taste the grilled morsels becomes a delectable pleasure with incalculable consequences. Those who eat are as mortal as the animals they kill and transform into food. To the gods accrues the best part. They rejoice in the sacrificial fumes, eat nothing, and thus enjoy the superb state of immortality in which human beings have installed them. Meat is eaten only at a sacrifice, and eating meat means reenacting around the smoking and bloody altar the very order of the universe. In this context, vegetarianism is subversion. The sacrifice begins with a procession, which is organized as a ceremonial path toward the place where the gods are to be found, at the altar or sanctuary where they await the honors of mortals (fig. 152).

On the belly of a large krater in Ferrara (fig. 73), we see the arrival of a cortège at the sanctuary of Apollo. The god, in his usual guise of a handsome young man, is enthroned on the right, surrounded by his attributes—the quiver, laurel branch, and tripod. Two columns mark off the area of the sanctuary. Before him are the human beings, advancing with dignity at the calm pace of the beasts who will be their victims. The first is a priest leaning on a staff, a man like the others, but bearded, older, responsible for the smooth running of the operation. He faces left towards those who follow him. All are young men, except the first, a richly clothed woman who carries on her head a three-handled basket containing the grain needed for the ritual. An incense-burner for the sacred fumigation creates a vertical rhythm in the space. Just in front of the victim an assistant carries a cup in his right hand for pouring wine onto the altar. The cattle close the procession. Nothing here suggests the coming death of the animals which is central to the ritual act. The fateful knife is hidden under the grain, in the basket (*kanoun*) carried by the young woman.

The human order guaranteed and required by the gods is thus established around a dangerous act which contains within it the seeds of a violence that could destroy that very order. This violence, then, must be kept at a distance to prevent it from contaminating or insinuating its way into the ritual procedure. The act of sacrificial killing is treated with discretion, being omitted, for example, from depictions of the ritual. We can take as our guide to the illustration of sacrifice the series of operations shown on the shoulder of a water vessel, a hydria in the Villa Giulia (fig. 74). It is not an Attic vase, but it carries the largest series of sacrificial operations represented together. We shall follow it to avoid the risk of giving a false picture by misrepresenting the rites of a strange culture which are difficult to understand. Later on we will consider several parallel Attic scenes. Sacrifice is murder, but death is not its object. On a small vase (*olpe*) in Berlin (fig. 75), one can see an

FIG. 74. *Sacrifice, from the handling* ▷ *of the carcass to the division of portions.*

FIG. 75. *Before the bloodletting.*

unusual sacrificial victim, a tuna, presented by an assistant on the right in the classic position for sacrificial killing. There is a table (*trapeza*) for the final blow, an altar to honor the gods, and a large receptacle to gather the blood destined for the gods alone, which the knife (*machaira*) will cause to flow.

The important thing is to eat together, choosing from the body, now a source of meat, the portions that will most bind the eaters together. The noble viscera (*splanchna*), seat of life and responsible for the unity of the living body, are gathered first. On a drinking-vase (*skyphos*) in Warsaw (fig. 76), one can see the priest, on the right, plunging his hands into the opened chest of a sheep, up to the last rib. An assistant, on the left, provides resistance, pulling in the opposite direction from the priest. They are most likely engaged in retrieving the kidneys, last on the list of *splanchna* after the heart, the lungs, and the liver. The body is spread out on the same table (*trapeza*) that will later be used for the second division of the meat to be eaten.

The entrails, spitted and often wrapped in bundles, are seared in the flame. It is then that the prayer, an appeal to the gods, is made and the libation is poured on the

FIG. 76. *At the table, gathering the entrails.*

FIG. 77. *At the altar, grilling the entrails.*

altar. On an oinochoe in the Louvre (fig. 77), one can see a young assistant, naked, on the right, holding a bunch of spits. On the left, the priest, his left hand raised in a gesture of prayer, tilts the cup above the flames. The pictures show cooking, but never eating, since nourishment itself is not the main point. When the meat has been cut into portions, it is boiled in a cauldron, the obligatory equipment at this stage of the sacred cuisine. One sees it on a cup in the Louvre (fig. 78), with an adept engaged in cooking the stew, holding the parts as yet uncooked. Each person will have an equal share, without special distinction. The cuisine of sacrifice means first of all equal access to the common supply of meat, an elementary democracy.

In the sanctuaries, a large basin serves for the sacred ablutions that punctuate the unfolding of the ceremonies. Symmetrical with the altar (*bomos*), the basin (*louterion*) helps to organize the space of the images. The oxen, about to be victims, take their place on either side of one of these signs of the sacrificial space (fig. 79).

FIG. 78. *At the cauldron, boiling the meat.*

The meat not eaten on the spot is once again brought to the table and threaded on the spits on which it will be carried away. The table is indispensable for the division of the meat beginning with the extraction of the viscera and ending with the disposition of the less prestigious portions. And the murderous knife hidden in the basket is shown as the instrument of the butchering. On an olpe in Heidelberg (fig. 80), one can see thus two sacrificial attendants engaged in the making up of these spits used for the anonymous portions which will be eaten outside of the sacred zone. Each successive cut of meat after the entrails becomes more "ordinary." Each person in the social collectivity is defined thus as having the right to a sacrificial meal by his place in the general sharing.

Herakles, for his part, is a hero who has no share in this rite. His superhuman force puts him at the level of the immortals and for him sacrifice is never a simple affair. On a vase in Boston (fig. 81), one can see him in a procession with the ox intended for the ceremony. This procession of one shows, instead of the peaceable

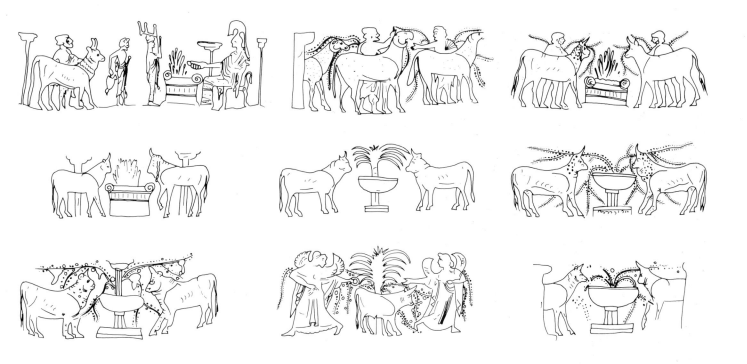

FIG. 79. *The procession to the sanctuary—concrete order and abstract symmetrical variation.*

FIG. 80. *At the table: threading meat onto the spit.*

basket of the classic parade, the packet of spits, which will hold the cut-up meat of the animal. Instead of the procedures of distancing which make a gradual transition from death to meat, Herakles proceeds directly without intermediate steps, from the animal on the hoof to the carnivorous nourishment reserved for him alone. An ox—and what is more, a whole ox—is given to the solitary hero who excludes himself from the shared community of human beings. Thus Herakles permits men to speak of the violence underlying sacrifice. This violence cannot be hidden, but if it must be given its due, only the hero of violence will serve. Herakles refuses to share and reveals the violence of this ceremony designed to eliminate violence. Even

FIG. 81. *Herakles carries the spits to his solitary sacrifice.* 57

more horrible, he is capable of putting to death, in order to feed himself, an animal very close to man, too domesticated to be eaten. And he eats alone: from under the very yoke, he devours the beast of burden, an animal but also man's indispensable agricultural companion. A violent hero for an almost cannibalistic sacrifice, it is imperative to get rid of Herakles; he must be divinized.

Even at the moment of death, the men's gestures are gentle and calming. On a vase in Boston (fig. 82), we see an assistant leaning over a sheep, his two hands lightly placed on either side of the animal's neck just as the priest at the altar is about to sprinkle it with lustral water and grain to obtain the consenting nod of the head. At the last minute, the peaceful grain is brought into contact with the animal just before the second phase of the ceremony, in which meat will be the only consideration.

On a large amphora in Viterbo (fig. 83), one can see—and it is a unique exception in the body of imagery—an entirely different way of presenting the animal to the sacrificer, a method allowing constraint and violent mastery of a victim of great size by a large group of men called together for this purpose. Bearded men, engaged in a difficult collective effort, form an athletic pyramid to carry on their shoulders an ox which they present immobile to the sacrificial blade. Here we see constraint, but not brutality, in the encounter with the beast. It is a strenuous physical undertaking, but one that ends in an athletic performance revealing in all its purity the solidarity of the men, naked around the animal they have now controlled and mastered. This is another way of showing the close collaboration, this time athletic, by which the group affirms itself, and the pacification of the ritual space in which the body of the beast is completely mastered.

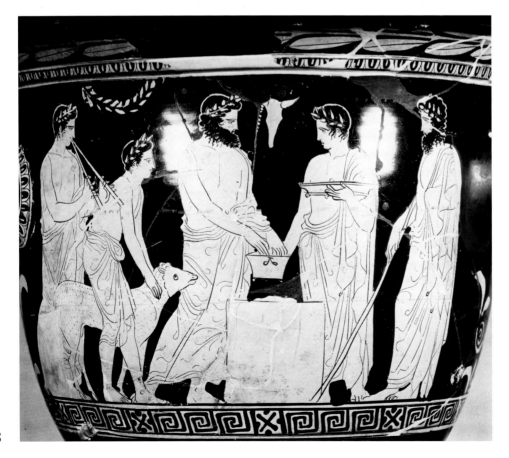

FIG. 82. *At the altar: the gentleness of the men and the calm of the animals.*

FIG. 83. *An ox on the shoulders, a manly feat.*

Mastery of the Domestic Animal, Capture of the Wild Animal

Sacrifice, as we have seen, determines the relations between men and animals. The rules that authorize it and the procedures that render it efficacious are the guarantee of a balance between men and animals.

Sacrifice is the domestic side of the control of animals. If they are wild, however, they must be captured and mastered by the techniques of the hunt which are fundamental for men. For wild animals are in a certain way threats and competitors for men. For Isocrates, "The most necessary and most just war is that which men wage together against the savagery of beasts, the second being that which the Greeks wage against barbarians" (*Panathenaika*, 163). If the war of Greeks against "barbarians" is the revelation of Hellenism, the hunting of animals is for men the guarantor, on the anthropological level, of human identity. For the Greeks, hunting is not only a simple matter of subsistance, but a means of affirming themselves as men among other living beings. In the myth of the *Protagoras*, hunting is the basis of the political and social life of men because it permits them to free themselves from the threat of animals:

Because man partook of the divine allotment, at first he was the only animal to honor the gods, and he began to construct altars and divine images; then he learned how to make sounds and articulate speech, he invented houses, clothing, shoes, coverings, and foods born from the earth. But the human beings, thus provided for, at first lived dispersed, and there were no cities. For this reason they were destroyed by animals, who were always and everywhere stronger than they, and their industry, sufficient to nourish them, was powerless to wage war against the animals; but they did not yet have the art of politics of which the art of war is a part. (*Protagoras,* 322b) 59

FIG. 84. *Between hunt and sacrifice.*

From this enunciation of the principles of civilization, we see that it is religion that separates men from the rest of living things and distinguishes them from animals. But this religion, which consists in honoring the gods, rests in turn on sacrifice (altars) and the capacity to give the gods an image. Because he knows how to recognize the gods, to name them, and to pray to them, man becomes civilized. Language, agriculture, and crafts are the immediate result. Even so, men remain unfinished. Once men have regulated their relations with the gods, and mastered the inanimate part of nature, the conquest of the world becomes the battle against

FIG. 85. *A branch offered to a herm.*

animals; hunting is in a certain sense the other side of war. The mastery of animals and the defense against other groups of men call for training, organization—in short, politics in the Greek sense.

Thus hunting is the complement to sacrifice, but in a very different sphere, not that which unites men to the gods, but that which organizes the relations of men with one another.

A hydria in Berlin (fig. 84) is exceptional in joining images of the hunt and of sacrifice. At each corner of the picture, a naked young man tames a bull with the strength of his arms. In the middle, two figures, back to back, watch the scene. They, by contrast, are clothed with the chlamys, armed with spears, and accompanied by a dog holding in its mouth the hoof already cut from an animal. Here sacrificers and hunters are one and the same.

Like domestic animals, game may also at times be the object of offerings to the gods. In dedicating a part of his take to Artemis or Pan, the hunter appeases the divinity. On a red-figure lekythos in Athens (fig. 85), a hunter dressed in a chiton and a chlamys, with a pilos on his head, offers a branch to a herm in front of him. On the lekythos in Athens, the hunter offers a simple flower, while on another in Heidelberg (fig. 86), we see something like a later stage in the same proceedings. Suspended from a Doric column on the left is a hare, and on the right above a stepped altar, a herm. In the center of the image is a representation of a crouching satyr. Once again, the painted image appears as the combination of a series of interlocking symbols. The column stands for the space of the city, the temple-colonnade, the hare is the absent hunter's dedication, the stepped altar and the herm represent the divinity no longer present but seen as an architectural element in the landscape. In the center is the satyr, whose representation helps bring together the different elements of the scene. This is a transitional image between the cult devoted to the gods, and the hunt, the pursuit not of a consenting animal, as in the imagery of sacrifice, but of one that rebels. For without the violence done to the animal, the hunt is not a true hunt. That which sacrifice strains to hide becomes manifest in the hunt.

FIG. 86. *Sanctuary: the silence of the offering in the hunter's absence, set in an architectural space with column and altar.*

The Ephebes' Hunt

In the Greek tradition, the good hunt, which Plato commends to the ephebes, is the running hunt:

> For our athletes only the hunt and capture of land animals is appropriate; one of its forms is the hunt by night, in which hunters sleep in turn, lazy men; this kind of hunting merits no praise. Equally unworthy is the hunt in which work and rest alternate, in which the savage strength of the beast is tamed, not by the victory of a valiant spirit, but by the aid of nets or traps. There remains only the most excellent, that of four-footed quarry, with the aid of hounds and horses and one's own body; and this prey they capture by running after them or by striking them from near or far but only by the use of their own hands, for those who cultivate godlike valor. (*Laws*, VII, 823e)

The hunt is thus conceived according to martial values which privilege hand-to-hand combat in battle formation rather than ambush and surprise. Just as war has its dark side, so does hunting, when it takes place at night, hidden behind the nets. This kind of hunt, the hunt of the hare using nets, relies on surprise and stratagems. It plays a fundamental role in Attic imagery, but has more to do with the erotic and the socialization of the young than with the imagery of the hunt by pursuit.

The noble hunt, on the other hand, that which corresponds to Plato's ideal, never makes use of traps. In the hunt for stag or boar there is no place for traps. Not that Greek hunters did not use them—we know from Xenophon that they had perfect mastery of all kinds of traps—but because the image-makers valorized the athletic character of the hunt: they made of big game hunting an art of "godlike valor."

On a banded cup in Orvieto (fig. 87), a naked hunter armed with a club runs with all his might after a fleeing buck. On the other side, another hunter, in the same position, but with a chlamys protecting his forearm, throws a stone at another fleeing buck. No landscape and no companions are depicted here; the physical encounter alone is important. The same can be said of a lekythos in Oxford (fig. 88). This time, the hunter, again on foot, chases a stag and a doe. He is armed with spears, one of which has pierced the doe, while the other flies in the direction of the stag.

The theme of hunting on foot, however, is too closely connected to that of hare-hunting: the noble hunt as understood by the artists of the sixth century is a mounted hunt in which a cavalcade of young men pursues the animal—stag, doe, or boar. This classic theme appears on a series of cups. On a cup in the Villa Giulia (fig. 89), four horsemen attack a stag, while on the other side four hunters track two does wounded by spears. What the image gains in complexity of composition, it loses in details. The hunters on foot, like those on the Orvieto cup, are identifiable; the mounted hunters of black figure are anonymous. The imagery of the hunt is reduced to a single dominant theme, the encounter of a group of young men on horseback with the game. The artist is interested in neither the equipment of the hunt, nor the dogs, the different types of weapons, the trappings, nor even in the postures of the hunters, all of whom are stereotyped. Only the position of the animal and the play of the spears, pointed or planted, introduce a minimal element of variety.

On a series of hydrias and amphoras mostly by the Antimenes painter at the end of the sixth century, the collective hunt of deer and boar finds its best expression. The hunting scene is not generally the main image, but is instead shown on a band, the predella. It is usually accompanied by two motifs, which appear on the shoulder and belly of these vases. On the shoulder, we find gatherings of the gods, battles, heroic exploits; on the belly, gatherings of the gods, the departures of warriors, young people at the fountain, or chariots. We may note that religious scenes predominate on the shoulders, while scenes tied to the collective life of the young (departure, fountain-scenes, chariots) are found on the belly. Considering these images together, all of them contemporary, one cannot avoid seeing a kind of "program." All of the representations are linked to the social and religious world of the ephebes. The main images are given over to youthful activities such as chariot practice or fountain scenes, while the secondary ones show heroic scenes, battles, or mythological scenes. This architecture of representation—a religious and mythological scene, then a scene of daily life and a hunting scene—is the clear projection of the mental and social universe of the young. The role of the hunt in this context is to accompany the other illustrations. It is almost never valorized as a principal scene, while the departure of the chariot and young people at the fountain are the themes that claim the greatest attention. This body of imagery is characterized by a certain uniformity, but it is the hunting scenes that show the most stereotyped characteristics.

The composition of the hunting scene is almost always symmetrical, with the animal in the middle, framed by two or four horsemen, or two hunters on foot. The hunters, dressed in a tunic or sometimes naked, are unbearded young men who often carry a chlamys. They use and carry no other arms but the spear. The postures of the hunters and game are fixed; usually the hunters are throwing their spears at the already pierced animal. The Leyden hydria (fig. 90) is a prime example of this

series. On the shoulder is depicted the departure of a chariot; on the belly an edifice

FIG. 87. *The noble hunt, which puts arms and legs to the test as the animal is forced to flee...*

made up of a pediment and Doric columns represents a fountain. Water flows from lion-headed spigots under which the young men bathe. On either side there is a tree on which they have hung their garments. Below is a "vignette" (predella) of a hunting scene: two hunters with lances converge on a stag already speared; on either side, there is a huntsman on foot with his chlamys around his fist. The stag turns back upon the hunters like a doe chased by dogs.

The mounted hunt is the hunt for big game. Either deer or boar appear on the predella of a hydria. On a hydria in London (fig. 91), a similar group of horsemen and huntsmen track a boar. The animal lowers its snout, three spears imbedded in its rump and spine. The artists do not distinguish between the boar and the stag. On an amphora in Basel (fig. 92), the two animals are associated in the same scene: the neck carries the image of four hunters encircling a boar, a stag, and a doe. This is a key image, a synthesis of different motifs that run together to show the profound unity of the mounted hunt.

FIG. 88. *...and then is vanquished by the hunter's spear.*

63

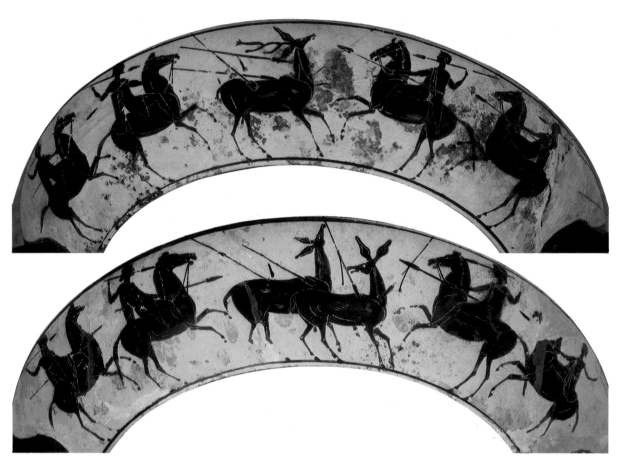

FIG. 90. *Main theme: a fountain scene. Secondary theme: young ephebes hunt on horseback.*

The hunt on horseback plays a particular role in hunting imagery as the incarnation of the collective hunt of big game, that which leads the young to distinguish themselves by their way of life, their participation in training and games. In short, the hunt on horseback is the demonstration of belonging to a particular group, an age-class.

The Heroic Hunt on Foot

◁ FIG. 91. *Boars and buck are of equal importance as game...*

At the beginning of the fifth century, the mounted hunt practically disappears from vase painting. Some have wanted to see the political consequences of the establishment of a democratic city, and lack of interest in a style of aristocratic life embodied in the young horsemen. In fact, the increasing rarity of scenes of mounted hunting is the reflection of a new taste, that of individual representations, of

◁ FIG. 92. *... and are sometimes hunted together.*

FIG. 93. *In contrast with the collective hunt, the individual hunt on foot in which the hero descends from his horse...*

FIG. 94. ...*facing the leaping animal alone, armed with a sword and club.*

heroic values which are better portrayed in the solitary hunt than in the anonymous collective hunt. From this point on, it is the solitary encounter of the young hunter with the game, the details of the attitudes, the postures of the animal, that interest the painters. Anonymous ephebes are still the models but they are more often portrayed in conversation or exercising at the gymnasium rather than at the hunt. The hunters gain in individuality, in autonomy of representation, that which they lose on the collective level. The collective hunt still exists, but not in anonymity. The hunters must be recognizable as the participants in some grand mythic adventure. Mythic creatures like the Calydonian or the Erymanthian boar are frequently used to emphasize the singularity of the event. It is these subjects that gradually come to dominate hunting imagery.

On a cup in the Louvre (fig. 93), the transition from collective mounted hunt to individual hunt on foot is evident. A young hunter in a chiton faces a boar. He is shown in three-quarters view, a spear in his right hand. There is in fact a horse in the scene, not mounted, but held by the bridle in the hunter's hand. The horse, one of the few figured in a hunting scene of the fifth century, no longer has a direct function in the picture. He is superfluous, accompanying the young man to his encounter with the boar. The horse no longer has a role to play in red-figure painting because he is no longer the sign of a particular type of life, the sign by which one recognizes a certain age-class. The hunt no longer serves to validate collective activities, unless they belong to myth, but rather individual prowess. At this point stereotypes predominate. The image on the cup in the Louvre is repeated twice, exactly, as if traced onto the cup. On another cup in the Louvre (fig. 94), the motif of the solitary hunt appears again, repeated twice. On the cup, the hunter, dressed in a chiton and a chlamys, with a petasos around his neck, faces a boar. He is armed with a club and a stone, heroic arms that recall Meleager in the scenes of collective hunting. In the second scene, the hunter dressed in the same way, but armed with a long cudgel and a sword, seems to retreat before an attacking boar. Moreover, unlike the boars of black-figure vases, who withstand the attack of the hunters with lowered snout, the boars of red-figure vases leap, with raised hooves, in a position of attack. The naked hero who faces the monstrous beast, is it Herakles and the Erymanthean boar, Theseus and the sow of Krommyon, or another heroic adventure? One thing is certain: the boar is no more an anonymous participant in these episodes than is the hunter. The tension that animates them and their solitude in the field suggests something other than the genre scene in which a generic hunter confronts an undifferentiated prey. The pugnacity of the animal, the plasticity of

FIG. 95. *Who is this solitary hero?*

FIG. 96. *Someone we recognize as Meleager, or Theseus, or perhaps even Herakles?*

67

FIG. 97. *In the fifth century, the hunters are no longer anonymous. Identifiable by their weapons, they surround the animal in a canonical position.*

the body of the hunter organize the features of this particular imagery. On a hydria in the Vatican (fig. 95), a naked young man wearing the pilos, and with a chlamys over his forearm, attacks the boar, sword in hand. Facing him, the animal springs, already wounded by a spear. Nothing designates the hunter specifically as a hero of myth; neither his arms, nor his face, nor his clothing allow us to recognize a hero with certainty. What is the source of our difficulty in interpreting this image? Why do we feel the same hesitation looking at the interior of a cup in Baltimore (fig. 96) on which a young hunter wearing the pilos, with two spears in his hand, attacks a collapsing boar?

The images of solitary chase are by nature ambiguous. Everything about this scene—its simplicity and its composition—suggests a mythic hunt, but there is no detail to prove it. It is as if in this period it became impossible for an artist to paint an image of a boar hunt without a mythological model casting its shadow.

FIG. 98. *Each hunter is distinguished from his neighbor by position, weapons, or dress. The hunt is no longer an everyday activity, but a mythic event.*

A transition has taken place from the collective to the individual, from the undefined to the specific, from the anonymous to the recognizable. The rules and values of the imagery of the hunt have completely changed in a few decades. The mythological hunts, and particularly the most famous—the hunt of Meleager—now predominate. The depiction of the everyday hunt showing ephebes in action is supplanted. Two images of collective hunting on foot, one of a boar hunt, the other of a stag hunt, are the logical conclusion of this evolution. In the scene decorating a krater in Ferrara (fig. 97), the boar is pierced by six hunters. Two are armed with spears and play the role of huntsmen. On the left, one of the hunters raises a club against the animal, while in the center, the main hunter, in the middle ground, brandishes an ax behind the boar, while at the same time, another hero facing the animal unsheathes his sword. In the background, a shrub locates the scene in the natural landscape. The position of the hunters suggests a kind of choreography rather than a hunt. The arms distinguish and identify each hero: the club, according to the mythological tale, identifies Theseus and Ankaios, and the spear, Meleager. The picture tries to present personalities, to reveal identities, and implicitly relies on the retellings of myths. But when the written tradition is lacking, the story can be read from the image. On a krater in the Louvre (fig. 98), six heroes encircle an animal, performing a sort of ballet around him. On the left, four hunters converge on the doe. The first of them pierces the animal with his two spears, and the others rush in formation. On the right, the first hunter is shown from the back, a sort of mirror image of his counterpart on the left, while the second rushes in, lances in hand. The hunters are equipped with traditional weapons: spears, clubs, in one case, even a stone. The clothing is limited to the chiton, the chlamys, and the petasos which they all wear pushed back.

What, then, creates the heroic effect? The context of the vase, but also the composition and the interplay of postures. Each hunter distinguishes himself from his neighbor by a detail of position or of clothing. These young men, so gracefully poised to track a deer, cannot be just any anonymous hunters. Their number and the care taken with each detail of their dress are sufficient to reveal their heroic

character. Unlike the stereotyped horsemen of the archaic vases, each of the hunters plays a role, like an actor. There are two paths to the capture of the wild animal: that of collective tracking, of the regulated exercises dear to archaic painters; and that of the heroic action which aggrandizes the hunted and the hunter by showing their common bravery. In archaic painting, these two methods are opposed. The young horsemen of the black-figure hydrias cannot be confused with Herakles and the Erymanthean boar. On the other hand, in the imagery of the fifth century, each image of hunting implicitly goes back to myth. The hunters and the game have gained prestige, but they have lost their spontaneity. They no longer symbolize collective anonymous virtues, but individual actions that everyone will recognize.

The hunt and sacrifice are two ways of recounting the necessary violence done to animals. Although necessary, violence is disruptive in a group that ideally conforms to the sophisticated procedures of democratic decision-making, denying the anarchic explosion of individual conflicts. In war the citizen may become a soldier, a death-giver, forced by the collective necessity of defending the territory, but once he has returned to the city, he must put away the attributes of armed violence. Like men, domestic animals participate in the rules of collective life, and like them, they must accept a controlled violence carried out by sacrifice. In order to be eaten, the beasts must die, but that death must be circumscribed and then erased. To get from the living animal to the distribution of meat, the Greeks designed a system that made this sharing the foundation of the city. The slaughter does not set up an order; it is a practical necessity. Attaining the animal's consent is not a comedy masking the horror of the butchery, but a necessary element to defuse the violence so that it does not pollute the ceremony and its participants.

The violence expelled from sacrifice shows itself instead in hunting. Here, the killing of the animal is at the center of the imagery. Here there are no complicated offerings, or subtle strategies—the mastery of the animal is accomplished by the brute force of the hunter who kills the game. Unlike domestic meat, game is never cut up for distribution. The hunters carry off the animal not to cut him up, but to display him whole. What causes uneasiness in the slaughter of the ox is its too great proximity. Distance, on the other hand, legitimizes the violence done to the boar or stag. Above all, the difficulties of the task, its ambushes and traps, are a proof of the valor of the hunter. To wage war against animals requires the violence repressed by sacrifice. To procure meat in Greece is to use one or the other of these divergent paths, the hunt or sacrifice. Woe unto him who confuses them.

For Further Reading

G. Berthiaume, *Les rôles du mageiros.* Leiden, 1982.
W. Burkert, *Homo necans.* Berkeley, 1983 (translation by Peter Bing of the German edition, Berlin, 1972).
M. Detienne and J.-P. Vernant (ed.), *La cuisine du sacrifice en pays grec.* Paris, 1979.
J.-L. Durand, *Sacrifice et labour en Grèce ancienne.* Paris-Rome, 1986.
J. Rudhardt, *Notions fondamentales et actes constitutifs du culte dans la Grèce classique.* Geneva, 1958.
K. Schauenburg, *Jagddarstellungen in der griechische Vasenmalerei.* Hamburg, 1969.
A. Schnapp, "Pratiche e immagini di caccia nella Greca antica." *Dialoghi di Archeologia*, 1, 1979, 36-59.
P. Vidal-Naquet, *The Black Hunter*, Baltimore, 1986 (translation by Andrew Szegedy-Maszak of *Le chasseur noir*, Paris, 1981).

CHAPTER V

Eros the Hunter

ALAIN SCHNAPP

The Hunt and Eroticism: The World of the Young

The ancient Greek city is a world of images, images on street corners and on the tops of monuments, on the pediments of temples and inside the buildings themselves, on the bellies of vases and on the backs of mirrors. Everywhere in the city are images that speak in the language of men. For the Greeks, every image has meaning because this city is a gathering of the citizens: real citizens pictured in their typical anonymity, warriors, young ephebes, old men and even women, or exceptional citizens, heroes who face the monstrous figures of the wild—men or supermen, but always men.

With an unequaled stubbornness, artists and sculptors adhere to the representation of the body that gives the image its own perspective. Archaic imagery knows no foreground or background. The space is instead defined and limited by the respective positions of the actors. The dynamism of the images and the effect they will produce depend on their proximity or distance. At the center is the obsessively repeated representation of the body and more than anything else the depiction of the naked ephebe. Because the city lives in and by the relations of a "men's club," the preoccupation of the statesman and the philosopher, the artist and the masses, is youth, always youth. Immortalized by sculptors, sung by poets, represented by artists, the youth of the ephebes is all the more precious because clearly ephemeral, and the city will make a religion of the incomparable beauty of the young who die in battle.

This time of life which makes living worthwhile must be depicted and told, made at the same time the example and the model of the desirable life. There is no other reason for the profusion of representations of ephebes on vases. The imagery is scarcely about daily life, nor about the city inasmuch as it consists of assemblies, meetings, political debates, or trials, but shows us instead young men at the gymnasium, on the hunt, engaged in various games in which the erotic has a large role. The world of the young, the ephebic world, creates a place for exercise of the body, athleticism, but also for seduction, for advances, for a complex and diversified eroticism.

The partners—the beloved (*eromenos*) and the lover (*erastes*)—vie in accomplishments and gifts. Winning the favor of a distinguished young man, being sought after by a famous man, these are part of the duties of any Athenian with social pretensions. The arena in which this distinction is won and in which the competition takes place is that of a particular way of life centered on riding, hunting, and exercising in the gymnasium. These activities qualify the young as partners in a social game in which youth is the most important quality. In this context, the hunt has a special role:

> It seems that there is no other pursuit more important than to gain an exact knowledge of one's own country. It is for this reason that the ephebe ought to run after the hare and engage in all other kinds of hunting, as much as for the pleasure or profit to be had from such occupations. (Plato, *Laws*, 763b)

The young man must exert himself in the difficult practice of the chase and capture of the hare, not to obtain highly prized game, nor to procure food, but in order to blend into the countryside like an animal. It is the Spartiate institution of the *krypteia* that pushes to the furthest extremes the implicit oppositions brought into play at the crucial moment of initiation. The hunt is an instrument of education, but it is an education that makes greater use of surprise, resistance, and endurance than of collective values. It is for this reason that the Spartan legislator

> discovered the hunt ... the hardening against pain which is practiced in all forms among us, in hand-to-hand fights, in thefts that are always accompanied by many blows, and also something we call the krypteia, an admirable source of suffering, in which they are forced to go barefoot in winter, sleep on the ground, and fend for themselves without any servants, while running all over the countryside all night long, until dawn. (Plato, *Laws*, 633b)

With its endurance, dissimulation, and suffering, the expedition in the "brush" is the crucial moment in the life of the young man which reveals him as a member of a group of warriors, ready to defend the city whenever necessary. At the moment of transition and the initiation separating childhood from adulthood, the young man must learn to be self-sufficient in a hostile world. He must experience a world that is different from that of the city. As he scours the countryside, the limits he confronts are not only those of the city, but his own limits as well. Whoever leaves the city and the cultivated fields in Greece is exposed to strange encounters. Fugitives wander at the boundaries of the city which, for one reason or another, they have had to leave: scandalous huntresses who defy the rules of femininity, solitary hunters with more use for Artemis than Aphrodite. The world of the hunt, like that of the erotic, is a space in which anything may happen and the hunter become the game, like Actaeon devoured by his own hounds. In Greece as elsewhere the forests are full of symbols.

Hare-hunters

The young hunters who appear on black-figure vases will be familiar to anyone who has read the exhortations of Plato. Here is a landscape rapidly sketched with a simple line, the dogs hot on the trail of the hare who runs toward a kind of pocket stretched before him—the trap (fig. 99). Behind the trap, the hunter kneels, the *lagobolon* or throwing stick in his hand. Here what counts is the game, not the hunter. On a bowl in Brussels (fig. 100) the hunter is miniscule, chasing after a dog and a gigantic rabbit. The artists have no interest in the landscape or the setting of the hunt. All their attention goes to the capture by trapping, but also to the action of the race. On a bowl in the Villa Giulia (fig. 101), the hunter runs behind the dog gaining

on the hare; in the background, a lagobolon flies through the air, while another hare cowers, caught by surprise.

The theme of pursuit is substituted here for the capture by trapping as if these images anticipated the opposition between the precepts of Plato, who wishes to require that the young hunt only by the chase and with "their own hands" (*Laws*, 823e), and the practical advise of Xenophon, who recommends putting the nets "in steep places of rough and uneven terrain" (*Kunegetika*, VI.5) in order to track the animal better. Is the hare hunt a difficult athletic exercise which calls on all the resources of the young runner in the woods, or an agreeable pastime made easier by the recourse to nets? The artists merely suggest an answer. In images showing nets, the hunters are superfluous, and they are almost smaller than the game; elsewhere, the hunters deploy themselves majestically, as subjects of the action and not mere netholders. On a cup in a private Swiss collection (fig. 102), two groups of three hunters chase a giant hare who eludes them.

FIG. 101. *The landscape does not matter; what counts are the weapons (here the club), and the animal.*

74

FIG. 102. *On the other hand, when the hunt becomes a race, it is the onrush of youths that is emphasized.*

Thus the attention of the artists progresses from the game to the hunter. On a lekythos in Vienna (fig. 103), two figures advance on a hare stopped at the foot of a tree. But the hunters are not running: the first holds back a dog and speaks to the companion who turns toward him, spears in his left hand, lagobolon in his right; at the feet of the second hunter, the dog leaps. As it is, this picture from the end of the sixth century represents an obvious break. Where previous images emphasized the chase, the capture of the animal, and the throwing of the lagobolon, the vase in Vienna focuses on the posture of the hunters, their clothing, and the gestures they exchange. Here are the timid beginnings of what one might call cynegetic sociability, a depiction of the cooperation necessary between partners in the hunt.

Capturing the game, but with what end in mind? The return of the hunter is a familiar theme for archaic painters. On the inside tondo of a cup in the British Museum (fig. 104), a hunter runs with his dog; from the stick on his shoulder hangs a hare and a fox. The hunter returns to the city, loaded with his game: on an olpe in London (fig. 105), he is not alone—the two robed and bearded figures flanking him represent the city toward which he is heading. An amphora in Munich (fig. 106) makes even clearer the uses of game. Young men are grouped around a crowned Dionysos holding an ivy branch and a kantharos. Facing the god, a naked youth pours an oinochoe of wine into the kantharos. On either side of him, the youths carry a branch of ivy and above all two batons to which are attached hares and foxes. Around Dionysos the young men participate in the wine-ceremonies, and they show themselves to better advantage for being hunters, capable of capturing the game as well as "running the territory" according to the recommendation of Plato. An element of social prestige and personal distinction, the game must be

FIG. 103. *The attention passes from the game to the hunter: the weapons, dress, and postures all overshadow the animal.*

FIG. 104. *The hunted animal must be displayed. Here the hunter parades with his hound.*

FIG. 105. *This hunter carries a fox and a hare, the same game depicted in the previous scene, as he returns to the city, symbolized by the two old men.*

FIG. 106. *Young hunters in the Dionysiac world.*

exhibited, manipulated in certain contexts, and the erotic, because it is at the center of the imagery of the city, is one of the dimensions of the hunt. J. Beazley and, more recently, K. J. Dover have studied the numerous erotic scenes depicted on black-and red-figure vases. Various gifts, advances, touches: erotic imagery is composed of complementary scenes whose unambiguous conclusion is a sexual relationship which is not censured but rather emphasized. On a lekythos in Athens (fig. 107), two figures, almost naked, face one another. One holds a cock, the love-gift *par excellence*, while he extends his hand towards the genitals of his partner. Behind them are pictured several figures of which the nearest on the right holds a stick over his shoulder from which two hares are suspended. The role of game in erotic court-ship appears in all its theoretical detail on a cup by the Amasis painter in the Louvre

FIG. 107. *The game—like the cock, a symbol of violence and virility—is a sign of distinction; it is the unambiguous pretext for sexual play.*

(fig. 108). Six couples arranged around the belly of the vase exchange love-gifts. On the principle face, a young man offers a chicken to a young woman who holds a flower in her hand. On the left, the erastes offers a buck to the eromenos who carries a lance and a crown; on the right, he holds out a fowl while the eromenos holds, in addition to the lance, a perfume bottle. On the second face, the young man merely greets the woman, but the erastes on the left offers a cock while the one on the left presents a hare. On each side, there is a bearded man, an erastes, one carrying a panther, the other, a chicken.

Considered in its entirety, the cup in the Louvre displays an extraordinary spectacle of amorous courtship. Four types of gifts are presented simultaneously: a crown or flower, domestic animals, small game (hares, deer), and a wild animal, the panther. Here we see the spectrum of gifts that organizes the world of amorous relations in the city. These kinds of gifts are, in principle, not accessible to the women who appear in this picture, except for those who do not hesitate to unveil their charms—the courtesans. The animals thus exchanged have value not only as indicators of spaces—the garden, the country, the exotic world of the wild beasts—they symbolize as well sexual desire and prowess: chickens and cocks, hares, and above all panthers, belong to the world of Eros. Moreover, the panther, like the courtesan, is a huntress who captures its prey with its attractive scent. To the panther which leaps, victorious, from the arm of the kneeling and ithyphallic man, corresponds the chicken calmly perched on the knees of a man seated on a stool. It would be dangerous to push further the iconographic opposition between an active

FIG. 108. *The full spectrum of erotic gifts—flowers, hens, and game—is here displayed as on a fan. The imagery is cleverly ranked from domestic animals to wild ones, like the panther, and mingles heterosexual and homosexual courtship.*

and conquering eroticism and a passive eroticism. The play of symbols, however, is by no means hidden, but in fact structures and determines the meaning of the image.

Game, whether exchanged, hanging in the background, or pictured alive next to the young people, is a determinant part of the erotic imagery. On a cup in the Louvre (fig. 109), the erastes and the eromenos make love. The erastes embraces the young man who holds neither a flower nor a crown in his hands, but a lagobolon; in the background a giant dog chases an equally enormous hare. The game is an unambiguous social marker, the sign of an age-class and social rank that gives value to the erotic relationship: the lover is to the beloved as the hunter is to the 79

hunted. The artist plays on the hunting metaphor with the same agility as Plato, for whom the philosopher hunts words (*onomata thereuein*) and is a hunter of the truth (*thereutes tes aletheias*). Thus the ephebe and the citizen are hunters not only for pleasure, but because the hunt is a means of expressing their abilities and qualities. Tracking small game, riding after the boar and the stag, participating in a Dionysiac ritual, exchanging the game, the ephebes find in the hunt a way of distinguishing themselves and communicating with one another.

FIG. 110. *The hare-hunt, mounting on horseback, the exchange of cocks and bucks, all make up a program of illustration which unfolds on the belly of this vase.*

80

A lekythos in the Boston Museum (fig. 110) is the perfect illustration of this social construct of the imagination. It is composed of three superimposed levels. On the first, in the center, an erastes accompanied by a dog faces an eromenos behind whom two youths carry a discus and an aryballos; on the other side, two figures offer a hare and a cock. Here we see a cycle of erotic relations very similar to those of the Louvre cup. The second register shows a group of nude horseman trotting in the classic arrangement of a parade of young men in black-figure. The third zone of the lekythos, finally, carries a hare-hunting scene. The hare chased by a dog throws itself into a trap; the hunter is not present but suggested by a lagobolon behind the hare, and on the other side of the vase, there is a cockfight. Courtship, riding, hare-hunting: three registers of the vase, but also three registers of the life of ephebes which converge to present a precise social representation. In black-figure painting, erotic imagery is thus a key element in the imagery of the ephebes, horsemen and hunters; the young men display themselves as eromenoi worthy of courtship. On the iconographic level, the erotic scene is the natural conclusion of the return from the hunt. The game is never displayed as something to be cut up and consumed. We must acknowledge in the artists' choice the deliberate expression of a precise sensibility. The game is not perceived as nourishment, but as an attribute destined for exchange and display. The vase in Boston seems once again to illustrate perfectly a passage from Plato's *Lysis*:

> Since my childhood, there is one thing I have always desired, for everyone has his passion. For one it is horses, for another, dogs, for another, gold and honors. As for me, all of that leaves me cold, but I desire passionately to have friends, and a good friend would please me infinitely more than the most beautiful quail in the world, the most beautiful cock, even by Zeus, the most beautiful of horses or hounds.   (*Lysis*, 211e)

The interplay between the images of the sixth century and this text of the fourth is clear. Can we nevertheless distinguish an evolution in the history of erotic imagery?

From the Wilds to the Gymnasium

Right off, the imagery of the fifth century is different. On a white-ground lekythos in the British Museum (fig. 111), a hare flees over the steep rocks behind which rises a tomb with three steps. Two naked hunters, with the chlamys over their arms, armed with a rock and a baton, encircle the animal while a dog leaps on the hare. The break is flagrant; the landscape so completely absent from black-figure painting here imposes itself by a kind of "collage" between the rocks and the tomb as a place of action. This is not a closely observed drawing which tries to suggest the "real" landscape in a graphic composition, but an iconographic composition that puts the hunt into relation with the world of death. This play of symbols places in the funerary background two naked hunters, in three-quarter view in the splendor of their heroic nudity. The tomb, decked out and adorned, dominates the scene, an indicator of the space become the frame of action. Singularized by this hunt carried out in so strange a context, the hunters are individualized by details, muscles, but also by facial features. The archaic hare hunt portrayed unspecified hunters in an undefined landscape; the hunt on white-ground lekythoi places the hunter doubly in the funerary context by depicting the tomb and by emphasizing the naked, intact body of the young man, frozen in eternal youth. The figures of the white-ground lekythoi show an interiority, an attention to psychology, absent from the archaic images. Here the chase is more important than the capture because obvious symbols such as youth and death dominate the scene of the hunt. The transformation of fifth-century imagery is not, however, one simply of decor. A red-figure

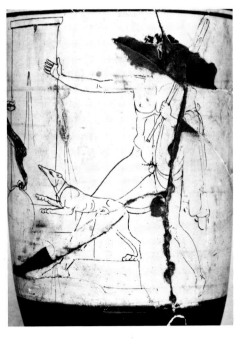

alabastron in Athens (fig. 112) depicts, on one side, an erastes and an eromenos entwined and, on the other, a clothed young man offering a hare to a woman who is spinning. The theme calls to mind the Amasis cup (cf. fig. 108) in the Louvre, but the nudity of its figures and the absence of decor is here contrasted with the clothing and the presence of a luxuriously decorated chair which places the courtship in a closed space. The woman spinning in her chair is the very symbol of the mistress of the house, the woman of the interior. This is not, however, a scene of married life, as the archaeologists of the nineteenth century imagined. The woman spinning in this modest pose is a hetaira who, by identifying herself with the wife, adds greater worth and distinction to her seduction.

The transition from nudity to dress, from the undefined frame of action to the interior of the house, is not the expression of a simple aesthetic experiment, but the establishment of a social framework, of different behaviors. On an amphora in the Villa Giulia (fig. 113), the bearded erastes leans on a staff face to face with the eromenos who is wrapped up to his chin in his himation. He offers him a hare, but this time, the hare, held stretched out by its paws, is alive. It is not a piece of dead game, an animal that has been chased and slaughtered, but one that has been captured and tamed. Gradually, the hare becomes less the prey and more the partner in seduction. On a cup in Munich (fig. 114), the entire decoration is consecrated to the theme of male erotic courtship. On its main face, the first erastes carries a cock wrapped in his himation, the second, a hare who appears curled up in his hand, and the third, a flower. If the position of the erastes is more or less the same from one image to the next, that of the eromenos is quite different. Almost entirely covered on the right, in the center he has one shoulder uncovered, and then he uncovers himself completely to the erastes who carries the cock. The picture proceeds by stages, by a mute progression that insists much more on the glance than on physical contact. In the second scene, the image is more static, but on the bottom of the cup, it is the eromenos who takes the initiative, reaching for the hand of the erastes leaning on his staff.

Thus little by little an eroticism of approaches and dodges is established, an art that makes use of shifting meanings and allusion rather than erotic aggression, that

FIG. 112. *The imagery inscribes itself within a more ordinary setting, entering the house, where a young woman, spinning, faces a youth offering a hare.*

FIG. 114. ...*or curled in the arms of* ▷ *a man who pays his court, leaning on a cane.*

82

FIG. 113. *Quite often, the hare is not* ▷ *dead but alive. Here it is held stretched out by the paws...*

suggests love rather than representing it explicitly. The image of the hunt as such is no longer desirable because it suggests the animal's capture by force, the violence of pursuit, and the animal's death rather than its taming. On the bottom of a cup in Berlin (fig. 115), the erastes and the eromenos face each other as on the Munich cup, but the erastes, carefully wrapped up, holds a hare on a leash. In short, the metaphor of the tamed animal gradually replaces that of the hunted game. On the sides of a cup in Tarquinia, several erastai court the seated young man, but on the

FIG. 115. *The theme of the hunt retreats before the taming of the animal. The two lovers face each other, while the hare, held by a leash, attemps to flee.*

FIG. 117. *The intertwined lovers are flanked on the right by all kinds of sports equipment—aryballos, sponge, strigil—while on the left is a cage in which a hare is held captive.*

FIG. 116. *Here the hare is no longer pursued by dogs, but still alive, it is held by the ears.*

bottom of the vase (fig. 116), the erastes seated on a stool unambiguously embraces a completely naked eromenos who holds a hare by the ears. Here the sexual relationship is not, as on a cup in the Louvre (fig. 109), equated with the chase of the hare by the hound, but rather with the taming, the domestication of the hare by the ephebe. This urbane, civilized, tamed representation of homosexual eroticism is seen at its highest point on two red-figure cups. On one of these, in Gotha (fig. 117), the erastes embraces the eromenos who, entwined with him, holds a lyre in his hand. On the right there hangs an array of sports equipment—aryballos, sponge, and strigil—and on the left a hare in a cage menaced by a leaping dog. Between this image and those of black-figure painting, we have passed from one world to another perfectly symetrical one. In the place of hounds freely pursuing hares in an indefinite landscape, a dog plays with a hare in a cage; there the eromenos holds a lagobolon, whereas here he holds a lyre. Even clearer, on a cup by Douris from the same period (fig. 118), the cage is open and the hare perched on the lap of a seated young man, cane in hand, is held by a long leash. A now familiar animal, the symbol of domestication, the hare (or rabbit?) is no longer a hunted animal, but a partner in the game, a sign of seduction and no longer the prey. The representation, from black-figure to red-figure, has changed incontestably. The clothed lovers exchange less conspicuous caresses, in a more reserved posture, within an internal domestic space marked off by chairs and stools. We might call these the two faces of the erotic—one turned towards the outdoors, the hunt, and the ambush, the other towards the inside, the gymnasium, animals caged and tamed.

84

Inside houses or in the vicinity of the gymnasium, the tamed hare is a clear reference to this new kind of eroticism. On the base of a cup in Laon (fig. 119), a bearded erastes, clothed and leaning on a baton, holds a hare by the ears. Facing him a naked young eromenos holds a strigil in his hand. An athletic marker, a *terma*, inscribes the scene in the space of the gymnasium and athletic contests. The hare of the red-figure painters is ambiguous. Without being clearly identifiable zoologically, this tamed animal, which is kept on a leash, held under one's clothes, or in a cage, has more about it of the rabbit than the hare. At the same time, hunting scenes are very rare in this period. On a kyathos in Brussels (fig. 120), three young men chase a hare. The first two, armed with a lagobolon, are accompanied by a dog, but the lagobolon is not used to bludgeon the hare as on archaic vases. The third hunter, leaning forward, seizes the animal in its tracks, holding it by its ears and paws. Having become a sociable and tamed animal, the hare is more like a rabbit to be stroked and caught on the run than an animal to be tracked in a band with nets and clubs. On a cup in London (fig. 121), we have come full circle: a youth runs without weapons or clothes; at his feet, a rabbit (?) matches his stride. What is important in the picture is not the capture but the race. The hare/rabbit is no longer a symbol of the wilderness, of ambush and surprise, but of the race in broad daylight in the gymnasium or the stadium. The young no longer return from their far-off expeditions, dead game over their shoulder, but instead display themselves crowned, with the live rabbit they have just captured in a race, as on a cup in Copenhagen (fig. 122). From the hare to the rabbit, from archaic initiations to images of seduction in the classical city, the framework of ephebic imagery has changed. Where black-figure painting valued the hunting expedition, the adventure outside the urban space, the red-figure images insist rather on the house and the gymnasium. An urban eroticism, more artificial and allusive, replaces the cheerfully aggressive images of capture of the archaic period. Like the city itself, the images

FIG. 118. *When it leaves its cage, it is no longer a wild animal, but a familiar pet which sits on the lap of the young man with a cane—the lover* par excellence.

FIG. 119. *Scenes of erotic courtship no longer take place in undefined spaces but in houses or on the sidelines of the gymnasium. The stadium-marker and the strigil in the beloved's hand correspond to the cane and the live hare held by the erastes.*

have changed and concentrate more on detail, context, and psychological expression. Interest is displaced from the fields to the doors of the gymnasium, from the country to the city, from the wild to the tame. The hare is no longer an inert trophy, but a live animal which shares the vitality of the ephebe, stripped down to capture it or let it go. The ephebes clearly install themselves in the urban universe, in an art of discourse that the images of the fifth century reveal in a variety of ways.

FIG. 120. *The hunt dissolves in youthful games. The young men are accompanied by dogs. They are not hunting the hare, however, but catching it alive.*

FIG. 121. *The hare is not a trophy of* ▷ *the hunt, but a symbol of the race.*

FIG. 122. *A youth prepares to release this animal as the signal for the race to begin. Is it a hare or a rabbit, game or a pet?*

For Further Reading

K. J. Dover, *Greek Homosexuality.* Cambridge, Mass., 1978.
G. Koch-Harnack, *Knabenliebe und Tiergeschenke.* Berlin, 1983.
P. Schmitt and A. Schnapp, "Image et société en Grèce ancienne: les représentations de la chasse et du banquet." *Revue archéologique,* 1982, 57-74.
A. Schnapp, "Images et programme: les représentations archaïques de la chasse de Calydon." *Revue archéologique,* 1979, 195-218.

FIG. 123. *Manual labor—the different stages in the production of cloth, a
"noble" activity which the painters are
fond of representing.*

CHAPTER VI

The Order of Women

CLAUDE BÉRARD

The Woman at the Hearth: Between the Heroine and the Courtesan

The status of Greek women, particularly Athenian women, confounds the traditional historian, who would see them as paragons of housewifely virtues and conjugal modesty, passing their time spinning wool, shut up in the interior of their quarters. Beyond this he might concede to them the right to raise the youngest children. This stereotyped image, created by Attic writers to contrast their women with the girls of Sparta who exercise in the gymnasium while showing their thighs, has been carefully maintained by traditional historiography. It is here that modern bourgeois ideology has found its classical references.

Although produced by men, the images painted on vases transmit a much more complex vision of female realities. While it is true that the means of production are masculine, the clientele for these vases consists mostly of female customers. It is to them that the painters address themselves directly, and it is they who express their preferences.

In the face of numerous images that do not correspond to the model of the type "housewife and mother," that overturn old clichés, archaeologists dodge the issue, either by assigning the women in these scenes a low social status as slaves, prostitutes, or hetairas, or by elevating them to the level of heroines, muses, or goddesses. In either case, they are denied normal social status. Must we say then that there were no respectable women?—that this imagery shows only an ideal world of male fantasies?—that the citizens, who were of course all male, related to women only at the extremes of more or less venial submission or of poetic and transcendent admiration? If we answer yes to these questions, we are lead into a succession of contradictions that can only raise doubts. Is it not surprising that so very many of the vases used by Athenian wives were decorated with scenes of courtesans? Is it credible that the homes of the Athenians were invaded by representations of hetairas, and that the women of the house would buy and carefully preserve these vases?

There are, to be sure, licentious vases that are the exclusive property of men, for example the drinking and banquet cups that each guest brought with him when he went carousing with his friends and in loose company (cf. fig. 3). This special-

ized crockery of masculine entertainment contrasts with that of the daily life of the Athenian home.

Let us examine the women at work (fig. 123). They prepare the wool, weigh it, spin it, weave it, and fold the finished pieces. The images show us precisely this part of daily life which field archaeologists, for their part, can only evoke by means of the spindle-whorl—in stone or terracotta—or the spindle and the weights that stretch the woof of the loom, or perhaps a metallic piece of the scale. Of all the other accessories—baskets, distaffs, spindles, shuttles, the pegged weaving-loom itself—there remains no trace, except under unusual atmospheric conditions. Such a scene poses many questions. Ought the frieze to be read along horizontal and temporal axes? Do we see here successive steps in the fabrication of a single garment? Is this a specialized workshop, or rather a house in which the mistress supervises the work of slaves? If so, how can we tell the mistresses from the slaves? By height, or by dress?

Here we must make several distinctions. In Greece, work for profit is frequently condemned. Working for oneself, for pleasure, so to speak, is considered a proof of skill, a virtue. For an Athenian woman, spinning is not a socially demeaning activity. As always in Greece, Homer is the authority to be consulted. Odysseus is an excellent handyman who works with his hands and makes his own conjugal bed, while Penelope spends her days weaving.

Not only that, but Athena herself, the tutelary goddess of the city, is a divinity of work. She has the epithet *Ergane*, the worker. She is invoked as the goddess of the skillful hands, the lady of the spindle and the distaff. Thus spinning wool means imitating the goddess who incarnates the exemplary model; it is to participate indirectly in a religious activity leading to the festival, offering, and sacrifice. The daily making of garments calls to mind the ritual fabrication of the great embroidered mantle offered to Athena to decorate her statue. This type of work has an entirely positive connotation. One should not be surprised at the frequency of spinning scenes in Attic imagery on the vases used by women. If this activity were painful and boring, as certain Hellenistic texts maintain, the wives of Athenian citizens would not have surrounded themselves with representations of it. The constant reference to a transcendent order charges the work with a positive symbolic weight which modifies its primary meaning. I do not claim that all labor can be explained in this way, but simply state that the Athenian artists do not depict unpleasant chores, of which there certainly were some.

We must not imagine, however, that all women worked from morning until night. In another image (fig. 124), they seem to be identifying more with the Muses than with Athena. First, some remarks about the architectural framework. On the left, the gate of the house (cf. fig. 35) emphasizes the intimate nature of the scene (we are in private, and not at the theater or the agora). In the center, a podium denotes a performance, a staging, or even a musical contest. On the dais, a seated young woman plays the lyre while deciphering the notes written on a strip of papyrus unrolled by an acolyte. On the platform, we notice an open wooden chest which doubtless contains other papyrus rolls of music or poetry. On the right a third woman takes part in the scene, holding a lyre and a box. This document testifies to the level of culture attainable by rich Athenian women. They are musicians, singers, perhaps even poets. They can read, they are organized, and they assemble to take part in entertainments of a high level. They own, or at least have access to, specialized libraries. We can see that parallel to the political space of the agora, where men's musical contests are held, at the Panathenaia for example, is the space of the home where the society of women reigns harmoniously. In the face of male society, women establish their own parallel cultural institutions.

Another image (fig. 125) brings us into the realm of dance. In the center, a young female flutist is seated on an elegant chair. In front of her is another woman in a long robe, breast-band, and helmet. She holds a long staff in her right hand and carries a round hoplite's shield on her left arm. The scene is framed by two young people. Above the flutist, there is a small bird-cage in the shape of a Greek temple (eight columns across, like the Parthenon, with a pediment and acroteria) and, further to the right, in the background, is an object in the shape of a cross which

FIG. 125. *Sports: dance in armor for women, an invention of the goddess Athena.*

remains something of a mystery—a spinning wheel, spool, or reel used to tighten the strings of a musical instrument. How can we identify the armed young woman who looks like Athena and is dressed like her? (Notice the substitution of the staff for the lance to avoid any mishap, cf. figs. 152 and 153.) The answer is given as much by the flute-player and the weapons as by the other pictures in the same series. Moreover, a series of texts specifies the cultural context. Here we are dealing with the armed dance, the *pyrrhike*, supposed to have been invented by Pallas Athena, the city goddess. Practiced by men (cf. fig. 54), particularly during the Panathenaia, it was also very much prized by women, who participated in it on various occasions. In the Dionysiac world, for example, armed maenads dance the pyrrhike (with a thyrsos replacing the lance). At banquets, naked young acrobats mimed combats with lance and shield. Finally, as here, a picture of a young woman preparing to dance plays on the formal ambiguity between adept and goddess. In this case, the dancer also imitates the city goddess, who first established this choreography to which philosophers ascribed educational value. Thanks to the accessories and the dance itself, the young woman becomes, in fact is, Athena, whose epithet Pallas refers directly to the dance. Her social status hardly matters. On the other hand, the cultural and anthropological aspects of this scene are essential: the spectacle is not a simple entertainment. On the preceding picture, the silhouettes of the Muses cast their shadows. Here relations between the women and the divinity gain in emphasis and depth. Her prestige reflects on them. These scenes are not acted out on a strictly profane level, and the sacred connotations are not negligeable.

Let us change the scene. Ancient imagery has made familiar to us young, naked athletes training on the tracks of the gymnasium (cf. figs. 53-55). The painters signal the gymnastic space by the marker showing the beginning or end of the course—the marker around which runners turn at the end of the track—or else by the trees that situate the action outdoors, or by the buckets and wells that supply water for breaking up the soil or filling the great basin used for washing. In the background, there is always the athlete's typical kit, with its sponge, oil flacon, and strigil, a scraper used to remove the layer of oily, dusty sweat that covers the body after exercise (figs. 126a-d). This is the territory of traditional male education designed to train the healthy body whose equilibrium and harmony are the reflection of the moral virtues demanded by the political order. In many scenes, however, the young persons portrayed are not boys but girls! How trustworthy are these images? Attic painters sometimes represent female gymnasts equipped for exercise in close-fitting pants, brassiere, and cap. In some cases, an inscription names the protagonist Atalanta, a heroine of mythology, worshiper of the goddess Artemis, famous for hunting with men and imposing a contest of speed on her suitors. In the classical period, however, Atalanta is represented as a simple Athenian girl without any mythological allusion. She is simply the model of the athletic young girl who exercises her body and claims the protection of Artemis. Just as spinners or pyrrhic dancers identify themselves with Athena, and musicians and poets with the Muses, the young athletes play at being Atalanta and invoke Artemis. In childhood, moreover, the girls undergo initiatory gymnastic training at the famous sanctuary of Artemis at Brauron, north of Athens, which was equipped with athletic installations for these exercises. In the image presented here (fig. 127), the young women are shown after their exercise. The one on the left, with a very athletic body, is in the process of cleaning her back with a strigil; above her on the right, one sees the sponge and the oil flacon—proof that the young gymnast's kit is not reserved for ephebes alone. On the right a young woman empties a hydria into the basin. A small perfume lekythos adds a further note of refinement. This does not prove that the scene takes place in the public gymnasium of the city. The column, in fact,

92

FIG. 126a, b, c, d. *At the gymnasium, preparation of the track for exercise: drawing water, dampening and breaking up the soil.*

could symbolize the domestic space of the house (cf. fig. 34). Here too, women would have benefited from an organization parallel to that of men. We must, however, consider solutions that might seem surprising at first. On several other vases, the column is replaced by a tree, an item we have noticed in the framework of the men's gymnasium. Moreover the gymnasium marker does not belong in a domestic space (cf. fig. 42). An archaic vase also shows us young women washing themselves in a monumental fountain which could only be found in the interior of a gymnasium. In Hellenistic times, the texts make clear that public baths and gymnasia were reserved for women on specific days. An amphora confirms that women hat both the freedom and the desire to practice physical exercise (fig. 128): in an idyllic setting, a creek surrounded by rocky cliffs from which springs flow forming natural showers, women dive, swim, wash, and comb their hair. They have hung their clothing from the branches of trees. But these trees are also hung with athletic equipment (sponges and oil flacons), which reminds us of the traditional customs of the gymnasia. The diving platform in the center shows that this is a planned space and that the scene is not exceptional.

Thus women's lives were less monotonous and boring, more varied and animated, than commonly supposed. While men discussed politics in the agora or banqueted in joyous comaraderie, women assembled in the orchards (fig. 129a) to gather fruit (whether figs, nuts, or pomegranates remains a mystery since painters seldom represent the plants realistically), or for animated discussions about flowers or perfume (fig. 129b). We note, on both sides of this cup, the alabastra, long perfume flacons from Egypt made of alabaster, and the unusual vase on a shelf to the left of the tree, which is important in the marriage ceremony and even more so as a funeral offering (cf. fig. 147). In this picture, the women's activities could have a ritual significance; the atmosphere that permeates these scenes is that of the festival. The participants' clothes are certainly not meant for work, and the baskets are of high quality. The young woman seated in the picture, seen head on with her feet placed on a stool (threnus) and with a flower in her hand, must be of high birth. All of these images present an extremely positive view of female society and of the dignity of women.

It is striking that Athenian women usually work or play in segregated groups. When a man enters the scene, we find ourselves in a brothel, in dubious company. The reality, as often happens, is less clear-cut; imagery enlarges the field of relations between the sexes without, however, devaluing the race of women (cf. fig. 179). In this subtle game, it is perhaps easier for women to leave than for men to enter the intimate world of the gynaeceum. Heroic mythology abounds in

93

FIG. 127. *Women's gymnastics and care of the body. On the left, an athletic young woman uses a strigil to remove the mixture of sweat, oil, and dust that covers the body after exercise.*

FIG. 128. *An open-air swimming pool.*

FIG. 129a. *Ritual fruit-gathering.*

FIG. 129b. *Flowers, perfumes, and feminine beauty.*

examples: Nausicaa, although a princess, goes with her companions to wash linens at the mouth of the river where she encounters Odysseus; Ismene, sister of Antigone, arranges trysts with a young man near a fountain outside the walls of Thebes; Polyxena, sister of Troilos, goes to draw water at the fountain where the hunters come to water their dogs and horses.

On the subject of the fountain (fig. 130), one must remember that for the Greek city, perched on its rocky acropolis, the water supply often poses problems. The best supply systems carry water from springs to fountains necessarily situated in the plain outside the city walls. Because of this, the Greeks often built a monumental architectural framework, at times sumptuous, in order to shelter the water carriers and to lighten the task, providing a roof, a rather high spigot (high enough for a shower), a place on which to rest the vases, basins to refresh the animals, and so on. The women (and not only slaves, as the literary texts make clear) seized such an opportunity and went down in groups to chat in these oases. Since their schedule would not be hard to discover, the men could easily find themselves there "by

95

chance" and engage in conversation under the pretext of offering their services. Certain pictures show that the scene could rapidly degenerate if an incautious woman found herself alone. Literary references confirm that the fountain could become a place of ambush and erotic violence.

When Women Put on the "Mourning of Love"

We are led into the domain of pure and private religious activities by several images often connected with the cult of the young oriental god Adonis (figs. 131-34). These representations confirm for us the frequency and richness of Athenian women's organizations. In them we find depicted a collection of rites and myths entirely controlled by women of all social levels, always parallel to the model of society ruled by men. While the key elements of the political sanctuary of the city—the bloody altar and the temple colonnade—signal the official religion (cf. chap. 7), here a simple ladder indicates the place of the action, a mysterious action that unfolds from low to high and from high to low. Propped against the wall of the house, the ladder leads to the terraced roofs of private houses where there will be placed small ephemeral gardens, prepared in broken amphoras (fig. 131), and offerings of fruit which will soon be dried by the burning heat of the dog-day sun (fig. 132). Down from these burning-hot roofs the women bring balls of myrrh ready to be thrown into large incense-burners (figs. 133-34). It is an ambiguous festival, centered on the image of the hero Adonis, the seducer with his aromatics— for he is the son of Myrrha, nymph of myrrh—the unlucky lover of Aphrodite, whose killing by a boar is the unmistakable sign of his social failure since that hunt serves as a rite of initiation for young men who thus pass into adulthood. Eros, however, is also present (figs. 132-34), and the young women seem to mime the mourning of Aphrodite (fig. 132).

96

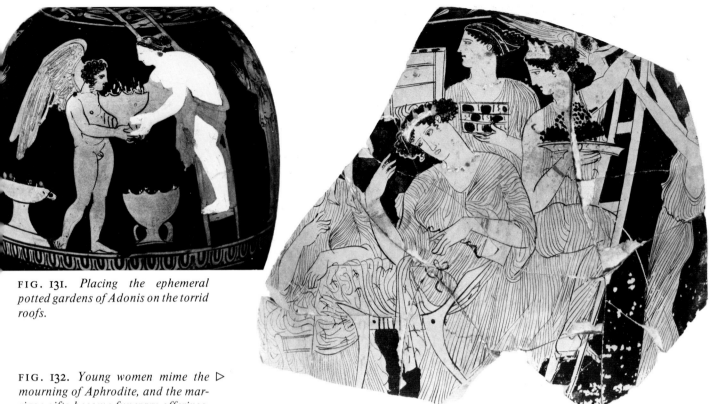

FIG. 131. *Placing the ephemeral potted gardens of Adonis on the torrid roofs.*

FIG. 132. *Young women mime the* ▷ *mourning of Aphrodite, and the marriage gifts become funerary offerings.*

FIG. 133. *The ritual of aromatics: a young woman comes down from the roof bringing balls of myrrh.*

The ceremony takes the form of a kind of counterculture. The pitiful and sterile plantings of small vegetables which quickly wilt on the roofs contrast with the cultivation and rich harvests under the protection of Demeter, the goddess of cereals (cf. chap. 8, The Mysteries of Eleusis). Just so the erotic (one might say aphrodisiac) relations, reinforced by the use of aromatics, are the reverse of fertile marriage in the order of the city. In the rite of the gardens of Adonis, the women remain alone. There is no exemplary hierogamy between the goddess and her male paredros, lost too soon, nor is there a heroic funeral for Adonis, this seducer who will never arrive at adult status. It is to be stressed that the image of figure 132 comes from a *lebes gamikos*, the nuptial vase *par excellence*, present in all marriage scenes (cf. fig. 138, behind the bride). Nonetheless, here the joy of marriage is transformed into lamentation for the lover prematurely carried off. Only a whiff of spices lingers in the air. Here we can see the difficulty of reading images and explaining rituals that emphasize by contrast the coherence and solidity of the institutions of marriage and burial fixed by the city's laws.

From Wedding to Funeral

Marriage and death, two important times in social and religious life, are pretexts for "stagings" in which women have the primary roles. In the archaic period, the painters concentrate their attention on the nuptial procession which brings the bride to her new home (fig. 135). She has taken her place on a narrow racing or war chariot drawn by four horses. Her head is veiled and she wears a crown. Next to her, the groom holds the reins and a long whip to urge on the horses. At the center of the picture, a masculine figure, similar to Apollo, plays the kithara. In front of the

97

team, another man is shown with the hat, boots, and caduceus of Hermes; it is the herald who conducts the procession. The reference to the religious sphere is thus clear. The nuptial procession for human beings is cast in the mold of sacred marriages in which the gods of Olympos participate. By comparing this with other more realistic representations (fig. 136), we can examine the use of this particular vehicle, the racing chariot, originally extremely functional but so little suited to its present use. The message, however, is clear. By its direct reliance on the divine model, the ceremony is shown to be fundamental to the maintenance of social and political order. Social coherence only exists with reference to the norm established by the gods.

The new couple is surrounded by a number of women who carry marriage gifts or ritual objects on their heads. We can make out, from left to right, a large round vase, a basket, then a winnowing fan, an object rich in multiple meanings. Functionally, the winnowing fan serves to clean the grains of wheat, separating out the straw and other debris, and from this comes its symbolic value as a means of purification. But it can also take the place of a cradle for a newborn, or serve as a liturgical instrument in the ceremonies of the mysteries (cf. fig. 21b). There is literary evidence for the custom of distributing loaves of bread to the wedding guests out of a winnowing fan. The presence of this accessory clearly places the marriage on the side of Demeter and consequently at the opposite pole from the gardens of Adonis. In front of the musician and the herald, two other women also carry wicker baskets which perhaps contain clothing or precious fabrics.

Another krater (fig. 136) presents a schematically very similar scene which, it is worth noting, introduces at the far left the priestess of Athena clothed with the aegis, the sacred goatskin fringed with snakes. To begin with, the priestess receives the bride and her parents on the Acropolis for a solemn sacrifice. Later on, she accompanies the newlyweds while giving them her benediction, whose efficacy is multiplied by the action of the magic aegis. This is exactly what we see here: the ritual actually inscribes the marriage in the order of the city and places it under the protection of its tutelary goddess.

On our last black-figure vase (fig. 137), the scene is more prosaic and perhaps also more realistic. We notice, moreover, that the chariot has given way to the more comfortable mule-drawn cart. The new couple is seated on it, the bride still holding her crown. A young man with a large pot-bellied vase has taken his place at the back

FIG. 134. *The myrrh is placed in the incense-burner.*

FIG. 135. *A great bridal procession* ▷ *on the model of a divine hierogamy.*

FIG. 136. *The great priestess of Athena the Aegis-bearer blesses the nuptial carriage.*

of the carriage. A second cart follows with relatives and friends. Two young women accompany the group. At the head of the procession, a woman carries two torches and leads the way to the house. It seems very luxurious, with two columns supporting a vestibule (cf. fig. 34). The doors are wide open and allow us to see a small serving-girl, also holding a torch, who prepares to receive the bride. On another vase, we even see the nuptial bed at the end of the room. The marriage then appears as a ceremony unfolding between two poles, the house of the bride's parents and the house of the newlyweds. The imagery faithfully reflects this transition—and this union—between two families.

In the classical period, the red-figure vases take up these same themes, with a slight change in accent. Thus on this cylindrical box, a pyxis (fig. 138), the standard marriage gift which, according to its size, may contain cosmetics or jewels, we once again find the cart and a woman carrying torches as on the black-figure lekythos (fig. 137). The same kind of cortège escorts the new couple to its home. A small Eros flits above the assemblage. Everything takes place under the sign of love. In contrast, the drawing on the cover shows a more static scene, partly real and partly transposed to a divine idyllic world. A servant presents her seated mistress with a coffer of jewels and a mirror. On either side, there are two specifically nuptial vases: on the right, the loutrophoros, a kind of amphora that contains lustral water from the fountain Kallirhoe, and on the left, the *lebes gamikos*, the feminine counterpart to the krater of men's symposia. While this episode is realistic, the rest of the composition transports us into the world of the marvelous. The many winged demonic creatures transpose the scene to a higher sphere. The groom, depicted as a god in his glorious nudity, holds a scepter. The other young man and the two young women who are spectators to this "glorification" of the bride and groom seem to be Olympians. Marriage is presented as a paradisaic adventure that ennobles and transfigures the heroine of the festivities.

On other vases, the nuptial carriage has disappeared and the scene centers on the reception of the bride. The image on this loutrophoros (fig. 139a-c) seems charged with emotion and tenderness. The young woman, her head hidden in a fold of her coat, is both supported by a companion and guided by her husband who holds her hand (in fact he holds her by the wrist, a very precise ritual gesture that appears more clearly in other pictures), while looking at her with tenderness. Young women follow with gifts (a large pot-bellied vessel, a basket, a flacon of per-

FIG. 137. *The marriage procession arrives before the vestibule of the house.*

FIG. 138. *Marriage as a paradisaic adventure.*

FIG. 139a, b, c. *The newlyweds arrive at the house: emotion and tenderness.*

fume), while in the house a friend plays the flute and a woman brandishes two torches of welcome.

Intimate scenes decorate the two jewel boxes with which we close our examination of this series. The bride is seen alone with her companions (fig. 140). However, the bed covered with cushions seen through the half-open door of the nuptial chamber calls to mind the bonds of marriage. The celebration is in any case over. The rhythm of daily activities reasserts itself. The bride herself, spindle in hand, stares fixedly at the reader of the image—at herself!—apparently lost in the deepest meditation. In front of her, a companion holds a small portable loom. The scene unfolds like a comic strip. Here we see the flacon of perfume, there the chest of jewels, then a large piece of cloth being folded by a servant or a merchant. The image presents an inventory of the goods belonging to the wife, the "golden jewels and precious garments" of which the literary texts speak, which are to be carefully distinguished from the dowry as such. Whatever the laws and customs, women in fact always retained a certain economic independence. From the fourth century on, monuments and epigraphic texts have more to say about the status of women. By the time of Plato, we find not only midwives, but even female doctors. Other women, even married ones, play the role of bankers for municipal administrations in difficulty.

FIG. 140. *From the love-bed to the realities of daily life.*

The last image emphasizes the architectural framework (fig. 141). We have seen that the average Greek house is represented at first by a door, with, at the most, a colonnaded porch. The walls are hardly ever shown, since they are made of raw brick, an admirable material for technical purposes, but not very attractive to the artist. Column and wooden door, on the other hand, represent the prestigious part of domestic architecture. Often painted and carved, hob-nailed and studded, these elements are a sign of wealth or even a work of art, reminiscent of the wooden doors of nomads or those seen on huts and storehouses in black African villages. The building accounts of Greek temples reveal considerable expenditures for the making of the doors, all in costly marquetry (the temple of Epidauros for example). In our picture the house is indicated by a closed door, some columns, and cubes that serve as seats. The atmosphere is festive. A winged Victory carrying a crown appears miraculously before the seated woman. On the other side of the vase, a domestic altar in front of which a woman makes a propitiatory gesture points to the religious meaning of the scene. Finally, between the door and another column, a young woman hurries towards a large basin of the type we have encountered in gymnasium scenes (cf. fig. 127). This time, however, there is no packet of athletic equipment signaling physical exercise. The juxtaposition of the basin with the altar

FIG. 142. *The viewing of the deceased on his bed amid the lamentations of relatives and mourners.*

pushes the interpretation in the direction of the religious. The exact meaning of the image seems to me difficult to determine. Without wishing to introduce anachronistic and rash associations, the Nike seems to be announcing the good news, the crowning moment in any woman's life.

If marriage represents life's promise, the other pole of family life is death. These two phenomena reveal, each in their own way, the coherence of social life. Here we find an almost equal number of men and women, united in the emotion of a communal event, whereas usually we see a feminine world parallel to the masculine one (even if the latter is often invaded by prostitutes, courtesans, and other hetairai).

The wedding leads us just up to the threshold of the house, sometimes allowing us to glimpse the nuptial bed, while the funeral makes us penetrate into the interior and puts us brutally in the presence of the same bed, where now the corpse is laid out (fig. 142). The two cushions of the funeral bed supporting the head of the deceased contrast with the large embroidered cushions of the bridal bed (cf. fig. 140). On the left, an old man with white head and beard, and his companion whose hair is still black, raise their right arms in an emphatic gesture of grief and supplication as they look towards the sky. On the extreme right, a miniscule female silhouette, a child or a slave, sits on a small block. All around the bed, finally, four women, the ritual mourners, carry on the loud lament—weeping, gesticulating, and tearing out their hair. In the lower register of this small votive tablet, a chariot race evokes the funeral games of epic and suggests the heroic aspect of the ceremony. Red-figure vases do not show notable change (fig. 143). We see that the vase carrying the image is the loutrophoros encountered previously in the marriage ritual (cf. fig. 139). Thus the function of the vessel changes suddenly according to the picture, and its contents, the water of life-giving ablutions, becomes that of mortuary libations. Here again it is the women who surround the bed, while the men are grouped on the other face of the vase.

Another black-figure loutrophoros brings together images that follow chronologically like the frames of a film. The sequence begins in the house where the mourners encircle the bed on which the deceased rests, his head on a pillow (fig. 144a). The scene on the other side takes place at the cemetery (fig. 144b). Gravediggers, hard at work, lower the bier into the grave where two of their number prepare to receive the weight from their companions. Women, continuing their lamentations, frame the scene. On the neck of the vase, we see other women bringing the sacred instruments, sacrificial vases and baskets, to the tomb. There

FIG. 143. *The women around the deceased and the men's funeral chorus.*

again, schematically, comparison with the nuptial procession comes immediately to mind, but the meaning of the scene is reversed. Wedding gifts have given way to funerary offerings which will play a role in the image on the other side of the vase's neck. In the last image, the dead man has been buried and a funeral mound erected, and the funeral vase, the loutrophoros, is left to crown the monument (fig. 144c). We recall that these vases were frequently bottomless, which allowed drink to be given symbolically to the dead as the liquid seeped to the interior of the tomb. Two mourners frame the scene, lamenting and gesturing. Despite the poor state of preservation of the vase, we can still make out the coils of a large snake painted in white undulating in front of the mound, while small souls flit about in the foreground.

The deceased is transported from deathbed to cemetery on a cart drawn by mules (fig. 145a), then, once the destination is reached, on the shoulders of his companions (fig. 146). This image completes the sequence. The funerary convoy has reached its goal—a great monument painted white, with the ditch dug behind it. Wrapped in a shroud, the dead man is laid to rest on a plank, with two mourners seated on either side. Behind the cart, a bearded man touches his forehead in a sign of mourning. In front, two other women gesticulate while uttering ritual cries. Once again, the women gather closely around the deceased and lead the procession. Meanwhile, guided by a flute-player, a troupe of warriors escorts the family (fig. 145b). These hoplites, companions from the ranks of the phalanx of the dead man, execute a kind of dance, with their lances pointed before them. The image unites the two spheres that constitute the life of the Greek man: on the one hand, the private sphere of women and the family, and on the other, the public sphere of brothers in arms, the political world, the city of men.

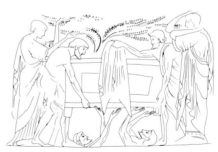

In contrast with this precise and realistic imagery of the archaic period, which is essentially descriptive, the fifth century prefers more symbolic scenes. The mentality has changed and spiritual preoccupations announce a new era. The voyage depicted is no longer that of the simple transfer of the corpse from the house to the cemetery. We have gone through the looking-glass. For the first time, the image of the dead man is seen in the presence of the gods. In front of the funerary stele, the silhouettes of women carrying offerings mingle with those of the dead (fig. 147). Here suddenly, the young woman finds herself face to face with Hermes (fig. 148), the god of passages, the conductor of souls who will take her as far as the boat of Charon, the divine ferryman of the underworld.

We leave the still-human space of the cemetery for the reedy shores of the infernal river (fig. 149). But is this ultimate voyage so terrifying? Charon, certainly, does not possess the idealized traits of the gods but neither, for all that, does he gri-

FIG. 144a, b, c. *From the house to the grave.*

FIG. 145a. *The funeral procession.*

FIG. 145b. *The city's last homage.*

FIG. 146. *Arrival at the tomb.*

FIG. 147. *Offerings at the funeral stele.*

mace monstrously like the demons of Etruscan art. Leaning on his pole, he resembles an honest fisherman who carries out his task without judging (fig. 150). More worrying are the tiny winged souls flying in this no-man's land, between earth and underworld, perhaps condemned to eternal wanderings. But, just as the funeral convoy is only the reverse representation of the nuptial procession, Hermes seems to embody the reassuring friend with paternal features who holds the hand of the dead young woman, veiled like a bride, conducting her to the final wedding. The dead are not denied all companionship. The mystery religions have provided them with knowledge and assurances for the beyond. Are not the coffers, baskets, and vases, scarcely functional in form, which are placed as offerings at the foot of the steles, the material tokens of these hopes?

FIG. 148. *The dead woman slips from the grave into the Underworld and meets Hermes.*

FIG. 149. *The underworld landscape.*

FIG. 150. *The last voyage.*

For Further Reading

F. A. G. Beck, *An Album of Greek Education.* Sydney, 1975.
C. Bérard, "L'impossible femme athlète." *AION: Arch St Ant* 8, 1986, 195-202.
A. Cameron and A. Kuhrt (ed.), *Images of Women in Antiquity.* London, 1983.
S. B. Pomeroy, *Goddesses, Whores, and Slaves: women in classical antiquity.* New York, 1975.
D. M. Schaps, *Economic Rights of Women in Ancient Greece.* Edinburgh, 1979.
C. Seltman, *Women in Antiquity.* London, 1956.

FIG. 151. *The goddess Athena in her sanctuary on the Acropolis, indicated by columns and altar, is represented as a priestess holding a ritual vessel. The owls are at the same time attributes of the goddess and emblems of the city.*

FIG. 152. *The sacrificial cortège and the procession of citizens arrive at their destination, the altar and statue of Athena, where they are received by the priestess.*

CHAPTER VII

Festivals and Mysteries

CLAUDE BÉRARD

The City on Holiday: the Panathenaia

Each month of the Attic calendar has at least one official holiday. In addition, numerous deities are honored privately by circles of the faithful, in more or less mysterious ceremonies. This is without counting foreign gods like Adonis or Attis, or new gods like Asclepios, the god of medicine, introduced at the end of the fifth century. The year is thus punctuated by all sorts of festivals. The Athenians go from festival to festival. A festival implies sacrifice, and since the butchering of meat depends in large part on the institution of sacrifice, there must have been sufficient opportunity to eat meat. The painters willingly place an emphasis on sacrifice, and scenes with altars are by far the most numerous (cf. chap. 4, "Sacrificial Slaughter and Initiatory Hunt").

Next to the richness and diversity attested by the texts and inscriptions, the imagery is relatively meager because of its selectivity. It does not provide us with illustrations of ceremonies that we are curious to discover not only as readers, but as spectators. Graphic and literary traditions generally follow their own paths; the graphic traditions emerge from a popular, and hence more authentic, vein, while the literary traditions have been seriously disturbed by intellectual reflection and the process of writing, operations that distort the transmission of religious phenomena.

The festival that most directly engages the entire community is without a doubt the Panathenaia, the civic festival of Athena, the goddess of the polis, patron of the city-state and its territory, mistress of the Acropolis—focal point of the city—on which her temples and statues have pride of place. The famous Parthenon frieze, we know, provides an image of the entire population crossing the agora in procession from the gate of the Kerameikos—the noble cemetery—as far as the eastern sector of the Acropolis. A large space in front of the Parthenon and the Erechtheum—more precisely, in the eastern zone of the latter—reserved for the old statue of the goddess, allowed all the participants to assemble around the sacrificial altar. The crowning moment of the ceremony was the reclothing of Athena in a new *peplos*, the sumptuous robe woven during the year by the young girls housed on the Acropolis, and destined to cover the primitive statue of the Erechtheum. The presence 109

FIG. 154. *In the framework of the sanctuary, the symbolic efficacy of the rites reveals to the spectator a religious vision of epiphanic character. The enormous owl expresses the divine energies at work.*

of this scene on the frieze has been disputed. This is not the place to discuss such problems of interpretation; in any case, the vase painters for their part never represented this fundamental episode of the ceremony. Here we touch on one of the enigmas of this world of representations. In describing and analyzing this highly structured system of extremely rich and complex imagery, the lacunae, gaps, and absences are even harder to explain than the isolated images themselves. Are these deliberate choices and rejections, censures, taboos, religious prohibitions, an order of values different from our own? It is not yet possible to give a complete answer: the imagery often remains silent.

The Panathenaia celebrates Athena's proximity, or even better, her presence and participation. On a black-figure lekythos (fig. 151), we see the goddess seated before her own altar, girded with the aegis, a goatskin fringed with snakes, sometimes ornamented with the gorgoneion (the magic brooch with a medusa-head), wearing a high-crested helmet, holding in one hand a lance and in the other a libation cup which she tips as if to pour the liquid (cf. fig. 21a). The goddess turns to look at an owl, her favorite animal, the emblem of the city, perched on her hoplite shield. The place of the action, the plateau of the Acropolis, is framed by columns signifying the temple, and on the right by the altar, the perch of a second owl. The image, as simple as it seems, combines disparate elements, showing the divinity in her familiar context, her home, not as a rigid and indifferent cult image (fig. 153), but as the priestess active in her own cult. There arises the first ambiguity. The role of the priestess of Athena is assumed by a noble Athenian woman dressed, as the texts clearly tell us, in the full regalia of the goddess, including the helmet and

110   aegis, which confers on her the appearance and all the dignity of the deity she

serves (cf. fig. 125). Thus the goddess represented on the side of the vase in a cultic context and in a ritual act of libation is a pious image that functions as an exemplary model for the priestess just as she, when dressed as Athena, embodies the goddess's majesty for the faithful.

A second image introduces men and sacrificial animals (fig. 152). From right to left, we see a mounted ephebe, armed warriors in full hoplite panoply, bearded men holding branches, musicians playing string and wind instruments, then the ram, pig, and ox led by attendants in short tunics who also carry branches, a priestess balancing on her head a wicker basket hiding the sacrificial accessories (cf. fig. 21b), and finally an official who conducts the procession and hands something to a priestess. The altar is lighted and all is ready. On the far left, behind the officiant, we see Athena herself closing off the image. But is it Athena or her priestess? It hardly matters here. It is precisely in this ambiguity that the religious phenomenon manifests itself. In any case, it seems that, despite the condition of the cup, we can reconstruct the gesture of Athena who is brandishing her lance in belligerent fashion. It this is actually the case, we are in the presence of a cult image. Such a reading could be confirmed by the panel of an amphora that shows only the procession's arrival (fig. 153). A priestess, dressed like the one in the preceding image, gestures across the altar toward Athena, depicted in the form of a statue, larger than life and brandishing her lance according to a sculptural type reproduced on vases given as prizes to winners in the games (cf. fig. 155a).

In a fourth picture, the place of the action is framed by two architectural elements—the altar and the temple (fig. 154). The painter has selected another moment of the sequence and another level. The animals, sheep and ox, frame the scene and announce the sacrifice. The citizens themselves are present in the form of a young man who makes a gesture of surprise and wonderment in front of a giant owl perched on the volute bordering the altar (cf. fig. 22). It is the same owl as those drawn on the first image, but with proportions magnified by the efficacious properties of the ritual. Athena has disappeared, at least in her physical person, and all her

FIG. 155a. *The statue of Athena represented according to the "Promachos" type—the one who fights in the front line—decorates the amphoras given as prizes to the winners of the games. They are shown on either side of the goddess with victory branches in their hands.*

FIG. 155b. *To the sounds of the flute, an armed athlete equipped with two shields executes a dangerous jump and lands on the horse's rump. The spectators applaud and award him first prize.*

energy is concentrated in the emblematic bird who shines supernaturally and fixes the spectator with its large, fascinating eyes. In contrast to the realism of the two preceding pictures, here the mediation of the painter and his picture brings us face to face with a religious vision of epiphanic character. The man is having an experience of a divine manifestation, a phenomenon of a psychological nature.

These four images show us, each in their own way, how the Athenian imagines and represents himself, as well as the episodes of an otherwise ordinary holiday. We may note the brevity of the sequence which is interrupted almost as soon as the cortège arrives, before the sacrificial act as such. The butchering of the animals is not shown, and the formalities of the liturgy are done away with. Priests and priestesses function as extras instead of performing their sacred functions. The city and its festivals include also the respectful silence of men, and the multiplicity of forms taken on by the divinity: a young goddess in armor making a libation, a priestess dressed as the goddess, a cult statue, even the divine energy magnifying the emblematic owl.

Beside the solemn processions, sacrifices, offerings to the goddess, banquets— episodes of which the painters show us relatively little—the Great Panathenaia, celebrated every four years, also included games and contests worthy of comparison with those of Olympia. Amphoras called "Panathenaic," filled with oil drawn from the sacred olive trees of Athena, rewarded the victors. A red-figure vase, which we unfortunately cannot reproduce here due to its poor state of preservation, shows the filling of these amphoras under the surveillance of the priestess of Athena in ceremonial costume. On one side, they are decorated with the statue of Athena Promachos, larger than life, shield by her side and brandishing a lance according to an unchanging type (compare figs. 153 and 155a), and on the other, scenes taken from the games: wrestling, footraces or chariot races, discus or javelin throwing, etc. Sometimes, as on the one shown here (fig. 155a), the grateful winners appear beside the great statue, confirming its character as a fixed and inanimate idol. These vases are infinitely more numerous than those in the first category, but their imagery is very redundant and monotonous, even across the centuries.

We have selected an extraordinary scene (fig. 155b), all the more interesting for its situation in an architectural framework. In the center, a naked and helmeted warrior with a heavy bronze shield on each arm is in the process of executing, to the sound of the flute, a prodigious and possibly perilous jump. Taking off from a block with a concave profile which serves as a trampoline, he seems to land on the back of a horse held in check by its rider. On the right, a naked man, probably a slave, uses a pick to prepare the track used for exercises, as is done for the ground of the gymnasium (cf. fig. 126b), while another builds a kind of scaffold.

The left part of this scene calls for further comment. Here we see several men seated in tiers and showing their enthusiasm by applauding. In the field, moreover, there is an inscription, the ancestor of the "balloons" of comic strips, which reads, "the vase (kados) to the acrobat." In other words, "The prize, the amphora of oil, ought to go to this one!" We might form the hypothesis that this is the tribune of judges who designate the winners. Another vase shows us the vases placed on a table next to the seated officials. Thus we have before us, in the religious framework of the Panathenaia, a picture apparently taken from life, which shows not only the performers but also the spectators, of some distinction, seated on a kind of tribune of honor like those we can still see in later stadia, for example at Delphi.

Does this indicate that the contest takes place in a stadium? A more likely setting for the festival in question would be the agora. Archaic cities often constructed tracks within the public space, which could serve as the site for spectacles of all kinds. The texts even tell us that on these occasions, temporary bleachers were constructed for the public.

Another picture (fig. 156) brings us back to Athena. The contest shown here, with horse-drawn chariot, is the most noble of races. A bearded charioteer, dressed in a long pleated tunic strapped across his chest (cf. the famous bronze statue in Delphi), with a small notched shield hanging in back, holds the reins and a long whip. On the far right, the marker around which the chariot will turn indicates that we are in the context of competitive games. Now Athena herself intervenes in the

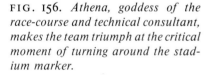

FIG. 156. *Athena, goddess of the race-course and technical consultant, makes the team triumph at the critical moment of turning around the stadium marker.*

action. Also at top speed in spite of her armor, she runs alongside the contestant and seems to speak to him. From Homer on, we are familiar with the role of the advisor in athletic technique filled by Athena, goddess of *metis*, cunning and calculating intelligence, a quality particularly necessary at the delicate moment of negotiating the turning-post. The message transmitted by the picture is this—that the victory will go to the contestant who invokes Athena and promises a sacrifice, in return for which she will instruct him in winning the race. Once more, the place of action is the agora, transformed into a stadium for the festival. Other contests, the *apobatikoi agones*, in which riders mount and dismount racing chariots in mid-course, are held in the same place, on the occasion of the same festival. We see that the famous Palio of Siena can claim prestigious antecedents.

Imagery thus shows two aspects of the festival corresponding to two moments and two precise and complementary locations: the religious sphere centered on the Acropolis, the home of the gods, on the one side, and the agonistic sphere, the contest, centered in the agora, the theater of human deliberations, on the other. In the cult, Athena receives the offerings of men, while in the games, it is the winners who are rewarded by the goddess. The Panathenaia, in short, celebrates the well-functioning relations between men and their patron goddess, the source of community cohesion.

FIG. 157. *From Athens to Eleusis: the priestess of Triptolemos in front of the magic throne of the missionary of cereal culture. This can only take place at Eleusis.*

A Spiritual Adventure: The Mysteries of Eleusis

In contrast to the Panathenaia, which engages the entire political community, are the famous mysteries of Eleusis, open to all those who are driven individually by spiritual needs. We know that no one ever betrayed the secrets and our few sources are difficult to interpret, consisting in large part of slanders propagated by the Church Fathers.

The imagery cannot, of course, fill the silence of the literary tradition. Many vases, however, carry scenes more or less connected with the cycle of the mysteries. If they do not deliver the quintessential revelation, the Eleusinian apocalypse, at least one can legitimately say that the episodes reproduced, such as they are, frame the decisive moment. By telling us what is not the mystery, they perhaps tell us a great deal.

A picture allows us to establish the link with Athena and her city (fig. 157). Eleusis is, in fact, a village halfway between Athens and Megara. It was for a long time an object of contention between the two cities, each of which tried to claim possession of it. At the beginning of the sixth century, the legislator Solon attached Eleusis and its territory to Attica. By tearing up the boundary markers, he annexed a plain rich in wheat. The ceremony has as its basis two elements: the procession from Athens to Eleusis and the cult of grain. On the tondo of a cup (fig. 157) there is a lighted altar on the left and a wheeled throne with winged axles. This extraordinary throne is that of Triptolemos, the Eleusinian missionary charged by the goddesses of Eleusis, Demeter and Kore, with announcing *urbi et orbi* the benefits of cereal culture. In theory, the hero is represented in the act of mounting his chariot (fig. 160b). More often, he is already installed (fig. 163), with an ear of wheat in his hand. We may note in passing the political import of this cultural myth. Athens, by its annexation of the sanctuary of Eleusis, presents itself as the possessor of the fundamental techniques of cereal culture, the promise of daily bread, and of viticulture (figs. 182-86), which provides the fundamental drink. Dionysos himself will soon have rights to the city of Eleusis side by side with the local triad Demeter-Kore-Triptolemos. In her bounty, Athens consents to let the world share in the benefits of these essential foodstuffs. The imagery plays a large role in the propaga-

tion of this ideological discourse.

FIG. 158. *The procession from Athens to Eleusis lead by the great torch-bearing priest; the candidate carries the* bacchos, *the initiatory staff.*

Before the empty throne, in place of Triptolemos, who would hold the ears of grain, a priestess is shown holding in her right hand branches (of myrtle?) planted in a ball of dough, and a scepter in her left. The extraordinary absence of Triptolemos indicates that we are not yet engaged in the ceremonial sequence. The little owl of Athena flitting around in the background puts the seal of Athens on the image and, moreover, localizes the scene at Athens and not at Eleusis. The episode, then, takes place in the Eleusinion, at the edge of the agora, the point of departure for the procession to the sanctuary. The priestess of Triptolemos faces the strange machine that will only become operational in Eleusis, when the hero sets off for other lands (fig. 163).

In the second image of the series (fig. 158), the procession sets out under the guidance of a torch-carrying priest, dressed in a fine tunic and a richly embroidered surplice, belted at the waist. A candidate for initiation walks behind him, carrying the *dragma*, a kind of staff made of sticks tied into bundles and ringed with leafy branches (cf. fig. 160a). This initiatory symbol, which reappears on numerous documents and often serves as a clue to establishing the sequence, ties the images together. Behind the mystes is a priestess with a long torch and branches in her left hand (cf. fig. 157).

A third image (fig. 159) brings us into the sacred precinct. Once having gone through the propylaia, the procession encountered on the right a rock-cut sanctuary, dedicated to Hades god of the underworld, who carried off Kore, the daughter of Demeter. In the first episode of the Eleusinian myth, the emphasis is on the rape; in the last, it is on the mission of Triptolemos. Demeter, in despair over the loss of her daughter, blocks the cycle of nature. The human race is condemned to die of hunger when Zeus, the master of the gods, intercedes wich Hades to let the girl go; she will however, not be allowed to stay on earth, since she has broken a ritual fast by chewing a pomegranate seed. She will have to go back down at regular intervals. But she will always return to the light and this return will reestablish the cycle of grain culture. The exportation of ears of ripe grain at the ceremony's end (fig. 163) corresponds logically to the reappearance of the young goddess.

In this third image (fig. 159), the painter has shown Kore on the left, coming up out of a crack in the ground. Behind her, Hermes, the god of passages, his caduceus pointed downward, guarantees the success of the enterprise. In front of her the underworld goddess, Hekate, seems to show her the way and to attract her to the gleam of the torches. Demeter watches the scene from the far right. Other images stress the realism of the ritual game while here we see an illustration of the myth to which it refers. This episode was played out before the mystai as they entered the sanctuary. The Ploutonion included a cave representing the gates of Hades. The priestess who played the role of Kore used a hidden staircase which can still be used today. It was a spectacle that established joy as the mood of the mysteries, the joy of a reunion between mother and daughter and the joy of the restoration of cosmic order. It is worth noting that the abduction of Kore is rarely represented. This part of the story was only made known by the recitation of sacred texts. One of the faces of a fragmentary vase found at Eleusis shows the chariot of Hades descending into the earth with the maiden, while the other shows once again the departure of Triptolemos, the end of the sequence. The mysteries focused not on the catastrophe of the rape, which is only recounted, but on the return, which is actually enacted. For this reason it is crucial to differentiate between images that simply illustrate a text and those which reproduce a sacred reenactment. In this way the pertinence of the distinction between myth and the rites associated with it is reinforced.

Already at this stage in the unfolding of the ceremony, we can see that a not insignificant part of the mysteries is based on a relatively simple symbolic mechanism, of the kind "unless the seed die" (John 12.24), expressing the sympathy

◁ FIG. 159. *The return of Kore: the young goddess has been allowed to return to the light by passing through a crack in the earth. Hermes and Hekate carrying two torches are the guarantors of this passage. Demeter waits for her daughter at the right.*

between men and plants. We must bear in mind that if the painters have let us see this episode, it must be secondary to the central revelation.

Having contemplated the return of Kore, the mystai probably entered the initiatory temple as such, the Telesterion. What happened there will always remain conjectural. For us, this is the true mystery. Karl Kerényi supposed, with great insight, that the faithful saw there a kind of "sermon without words" centered on the showing of an ear or blade of wheat. Moreover, several tableaux may have shown Pluto beside the two goddesses, depicted not as terrifying divinity of the Underworld, but as dispenser of abundance and perhaps even as father of a divine infant. Pierre Lévêque has emphasized the importance of hierogamies, sacred

FIG. 160a. *Two initiates in the presence of a torch-bearing priest, each holding the staff of the mysteries. The club calls to mind that Herakles was a model initiate.*

FIG. 160b. *Triptolemos, having received the ears of grain from the Eleusinian goddesses, Demeter and Kore, mounts his winged throne.*

marriages between divinities, which play an essential role not only in mysteries and even official cults, but also in ordinary marriage ceremonies. These divine unions serve as the model for human weddings. The imagery itself, on the level of representation, tends to suppress the distinction and to show the nuptial procession in a transcendent form (cf. fig. 135). In the Eleusinian scenes, the imagery seems to distinguish between the various hierogamies of Demeter, that with Iasion "on a thrice plowed furrow" the fruit of which is Ploutos, allegory of wealth, often shown in or with a cornucopia, and that with Zeus, the more secret, which gives birth to Brimos, a sacred infant who belongs to the central revelation of the Mysteries. To the extent that our hypotheses are correct, it was wealth, abundance, happiness, life, and afterlife that were exalted. After having "experienced" various impressions of this type, *experienced* and *not learned* as the texts indicate, the initiates no longer feared death: they "know," and they are "blessed." Of all this, the image-makers have left no witness, or only in so allusive a fashion that it is impossible to come away with any certainties. Perhaps these precepts were conceived as inexpressable in images? In any case, this silence is highly significant.

Some images allow us to circle around the central revelation. On a small goblet (fig. 160a), two candidates flank a torch-bearing priest. We note the initiatory staves (*dragmata*) they carry in their left hands. With the right hand, they trace a gesture of surprise as if they were put in the presence of an unexpected sight (cf. fig. 154 above). The large club placed in the background is an interesting detail identifying

◁ FIG. 161. *A procession of initiates led by torch-bearing priest and priestess goes to venerate the two Eleusinian goddesses.*

FIG. 162. *The ritual of torches surrounding Demeter.*

the man on the right as Herakles, the conqueror of monsters, presented here as the typical initiate. In fact, nothing aside from this artificially introduced symbol distinguishes him from any Athenian citizen. From the fifth century on, the cycle of Herakles myths begins to generate moral connotations. The hero becomes more human and accessible: he is subjected to hard trials which he meets with courage, he suffers and commits crimes, and he must undergo purification in order to be admitted to Eleusis. In short, he embodies the human condition. The image shows that a sinner may aspire to the benefits of Eleusis. Not only that, Herakles was a foreigner and had to be adopted by an Athenian in order to be initiated, as will the Romans later. Thus even a foreigner can be admitted to the knowledge of mysteries. This image helps us to gauge the difference between the Panathenaia and the mysteries of Eleusis.

On the reverse of this same vase (fig. 160b), Triptolemos takes leave of Demeter and Kore. He has received the sacred ears of grain and prepares to fly away on his magic throne. This episode marks the conclusion of the ceremonies. Here again we may note the ambiguity of the scene in which the actors represent at the same time the gods and their own priests. The figurative divergences between the images deserve to be emphasized. We may compare the priestess of Triptolemos in figure 157 to the priestess of Demeter in figure 160b who covers her head with her mantle.

We see how these images can be deciphered. On this last vase, the scene centered around Herakles (fig. 160a) precedes the one introducing Triptolemos (fig. 160b). But the imagery also functions in a more general way, each image recalling all the others by a process of association. Thus figure 158 precedes figure 160a in the same way that 160b precedes 163; figure 159 can only come between 158 and 161 or 162. Little by little a kind of pictorial narrative is reconstructed which had no actual existence in antiquity but which we have the privilege of bringing out. This approach of creating a sequence allows us at times to attain a very coherent vision of the phenomena under study. Let us consider another document (fig. 161), not a vase but a terracotta votive plaque, found on the site at Eleusis, offered to Demeter and Kore by a woman named Niinnion, according to the graffito incised along the bottom edge. In the middle of the lower register, under an altar in the shape of an omphalos, two initiatory staves crossed one over the other establish a sequence with figures 158 and 160a. A group of figures crowned with myrtle and holding branches heads towards the two goddesses seated at the right, shown larger than life. The two women in the group carry on their heads ritual vessels whose tops are decorated with branches. A young man carries a pitcher provided to refill the libation cups. Between the mystai on the left and the goddesses on the right, we can make out a priest below and priestess above, both carrying torches. They serve as intermediaries between the gods and mortals. The goddesses on the right seem to welcome the faithful, while the one in the lower register holds the flat cup used for ritual libations (cf. fig. 151). The image is noteworthy because it shows a large number of figures in a small space—worshipers, the priests who lead and initiate them, goddesses (whose roles are played by priestesses). We may guess that one of the important moments in the ceremony consisted precisely in the face-to-face encounter with the reunited goddesses, an encounter made even more impressive by the manipulation of the torches—one of which the priest points toward the ground. In the pediment there are other mystai, among them a young woman also carrying a sacred vase on her head, a flute-girl, and a bearded man with a pitcher.

Images of this type are rare. Their content is generally less narrative, the action more static and synthetic. On a hydria (fig. 162), Demeter, seated at the center of the image, focuses all attention on herself alone. She is framed by two torchbearers, a young woman on the right and a young man on the left. Their torches cross above the head of the goddess. On the right, Herakles, the exemplary mystes, calmly contemplates the scene. On many vases of this type, symbolic ears of grain rise above the figures, reminding us that wheat is always at the center of the mysteries.

A final image shows the departure of Triptolemos (fig. 163). He is already installed on the throne, holding the scepter, the ears of grain, and a phiale. Before him stands a young woman with the pitcher for libation and a torch. Two others hold flat ritual cups. Four women show the ears of grain, as does Triptolemos. Behind him, a priestess points her torch above the hero's head (cf. fig. 162). We are apparently in the presence of the closing ritual of the festival, in which the ears and libations seem to have an important place. We note that two male dignitaries participate in the scene, the one on the right holding a branch with his scepter. Aside from Triptolemos, no other man ever holds the ears of grain; this role always devolves onto the priestesses. Among them, we call attention to the one at the far right, next to the altar, who unveils herself as she carries out a ritual gesture, possibly recalling one of the hierogamies mentioned above. A column on the left indicates a temple (the Telesterion?) while the altar places the scene of departure outside. If one compares this image with the cup tondo (fig. 157) analyzed above, one can see the richness and complexity of the ceremony whose celebration began with the departure from Athens.

The secret of the mysteries remains hidden. But the specificity of the ritual is all the more striking when compared to the nature of the sacrifices performed at the heart of the Panathenaia. At Athens, animals are sacrificed; at Eleusis, wheat. At Athens, the cult is relatively simple; at Eleusis, there is a succession of extremely varied episodes presented by a large number of clergy, a complicated liturgy, with multiple accessories (torches, initiatory staves, specially shaped sacred vases,

branches). At Athens, the proximity of the patron goddess of the city has an epiphanic character, to be sure. But at Eleusis, there is the long history of a girl abducted to the Underworld and allowed to return to her mother after a terrifying experience—a kind of sacred union with the master of the Beyond—a dramatic story, perhaps explained by the metaphor of the wheat which produces its superb ears, symbols of cyclical life and of ever-renewed abundance.

FIG. 163. *The last episode in the sequence: libations in honor of Triptolemos' departure and the multiplication, exaltation, and glorification of the ears of grain.*

For Further Reading

C. Bérard, "Apocalypses éleusiniennes" in *Apocalypses et voyages dans l'au-delà*, ed. C. Kappler. Paris, 1987.
C. Bérard, "La lumière et le faisceau: images du rituel éleusinien." *Recherches et documents du centre Thomas More* 48, 1985, 17-33.
C. Bron, "La gent ailée d'Athéna Polias" in *L'image en jeux*, ed. by C. and E. Bérard. Lausanne, 1988.
K. Kerényi, *Eleusis*. New York, 1967.
P. Lévêque, "Structures imaginaires et fonctionnement des mystères grecs." Studi storico-religiosi VI, 1-2, 1982, 185-208.
H. W. Parke, *Festivals of the Athenians.* London, 1977.
L. Séchan and P. Lévêque, *Les grandes divinités de la Grèce.* Paris, 1966.
E. Simon, *Festivals of Attica.* Madison, 1983.

CHAPTER VIII

Wine: Human and Divine

JEAN-LOUIS DURAND,

FRANÇOISE FRONTISI-DUCROUX AND

FRANÇOIS LISSARRAGUE

Wine is a gift from Dionysos, who taught men how to use it. A product of the exuberant vine, which must be pruned, and whose growth requires direction, this beverage must be tamed and cannot be drunk without precautions. Only Dionysos can drink it without risk in its wild unmixed state. Human beings, on the other hand, can only approach this drug by controlling it with a body of laws defining the proper use of wine within the framework of a regulated conviviality. The very vases that are the instruments of mixing and distribution of the wine illustrate these practices and the god who commands them. Dionysos occupies a far more important place in Attic iconography than the one accorded him among the Olympians, where he plays the role of the stranger, the latecomer. Marginal on Olympos, Dionysos appears among men, in their daily environment, on the sides of kraters, in the bottoms of cups, beneath the reflections of the wine.

Dionysiac imagery is displayed on two levels. On one level, the painters show a society of men singing, dancing, and drinking, processions of joyous revelers, or assemblies of banqueters sprawled on their couches. On the other, they transport us to a parallel universe, a world of images in which anything is possible, where the human norm is inverted, an exception proving the rule. Satyrs have an essential place in this universe, taking on, in order to play with them, the various contradictions between animal and man, the crudest savagery and the most breathtaking agility. By their extravagant gestures, they pervert human behavior and reveal its functioning.

Thus two complementary procedures suggest themselves. One might move from the wine being brought to join the procession of drinkers (the *komos*) to the fixed banquet where everyone drinks and sings in unison (the *symposion*), thus traversing first the human world, and only then its Dionysiac parallel. The other possible procedure would be to move from one world to the other, image by image, in order to grasp the deforming play of the mirror which operates between the two kinds of wine, that of humans and that of the god.

Water and Women (fig. 164)

The most frequent feminine activity, of which the imagery offers multiple examples, is that of going to the fountain to fetch the water necessary for domestic life. This motif leads the painter to give more than usual importance to the architectural space. The building, with its columns, its roof punctuated by guttae, and its lion's mouth serving as a spout, plays an essential role in the image. It marks the meeting-point, the place of exchanges, where the women come together in an urban space, just as the men meet in the public square.

The spout here dispenses its water into a vase with a vertical handle whose Greek name hydria, "water receptacle," clearly indicates its special function. In front of the fountain, a woman waits calmly for the vase to be filled. With her right hand she stretches a flower towards the flowing water. This is the characteristic gesture, in these images, to express the exaltation of beauty.

165

164

166 ▷

167

The Satyr and his Fountain (fig. 165)

Leaping towards the lion's head which spits out its liquid is an unmistakably masculine figure with a bald head and the ears and tail of a horse. This hybrid, half man and half animal, is a satyr, one of the male companions of Dionysos. Erupting in this way into the world of woman, he upsets the expected scenario: the building is an ordinary-enough fountain, but the satyr does not stretch forth his hand towards the usual hydria, but towards an amphora being filled with a liquid that can only be wine. The fountain of wine is one of the miraculous places in the Dionysiac universe. The story goes that King Midas, in order to capture Silenus and wrest from him the secret of the wisdom he was said to possess, lured him by making wine flow from a fountain. It was also beside a similar fountain that Dionysos, so the tale goes, took advantage of a wild young girl, raping her once she had fallen asleep under the effects of the tricky drink.

The two fountains almost meet back-to-back under the handle, and the two scenes are symmetrical like an image and its double in the mirror. The wine of the satyrs casts its disquieting reflection over the water carried by the women.

122

123

Women and Wine (*fig.* 166)

The women of Athens retain their decorum even when drinking wine, this maleficent beverage that is, in principle, forbidden them. They only indulge under the powerful protection of the god who has taught them how to mix it and use it with discretion. In its pure form, this drink is a fire, a poison that causes insanity. It must be tamed, mixed with water in precise proportions, the chosen ratio of wine to water signaling the moderation or intemperance of the drinker.

Here we see women in front of the effigy of Dionysos—a mask shown frontally, crowned with ivy and surrounded by branches, suspended from a pillar covered with a long robe. Under the attentive glance that controls their movements, they soberly ladle the wine into goblets, which are of course destined for the men. One of them, saluting the god, is already moving off with a full cup towards some nearby banquet. On a table placed in front of the image, a pile of round loaves is framed by a pair of stamnoi, lidded amphoras, whose form reproduces that of the vase carrying the image.

The Wine and the Satyr (*fig.* 167)

The satyr, whose intrusion into the scene changes water to wine, may also sneak into the mixing place. We see him crouching behind a large krater with his head sticking out. His hand is raised in a gesture of greeting or perhaps of amazement. One of his companions stands on the right. On the far left, closing off the image, the rigid idol of the god, who has supervised the taming of the wine, is enveloped in a narrow robe. This mask, however, is shown in profile like an ordinary face. It is the satyr with his flat face and pointed ears who fixes his astonished gaze on the spectator. In its central position, this strange face, itself become a mask, focuses on itself and on the wine vessel over which it hangs the ambiguous and fascinating values of frontality (cf. chap. 10).

The Youth and the Wineskin (*fig.* 168)

A youth advances, captured in his banqueter's nudity, crowned with ivy, as for any feast. He holds in one hand a wineskin, also wreathed, containing pure wine; in the other he holds a skyphos, the goblet from which one drinks the diluted wine. From one vessel to the other a transformation occurs—the mixing that renders the wine fit for human consumption.

The Krater and the Satyr (*fig.* 169)

Dressed in a panther skin, which makes him all the more savage, a satyr walks while turning around, as if to look at the ephebe on the opposite face. He carries a crowned krater. The central instrument of the symposium, in which the wine and water are mixed, is being brought to be placed among the guests. In the other hand the satyr holds a drinking horn (rhyton), the emblematic vase of Dionysos, from which the god himself drinks pure wine, without the risk of madness which human beings face.

The satyr plays no role in the domestication of the wine; presenting in this way the two contrasting receptacles, he makes clear the double status of wine, pure for the god, cut with water for men.

168   169

The Komasts (fig. 170)

Sixteen figures are depicted on this cup, forming an agitated parade of drinkers. This troupe of revelers (komasts) is composed almost entirely of men, both young and adult, with the exception of the flute-girl who seems to be leading the dance. Wine, dance, and music: these are the three fundamental elements of the komos.

The scene is organized as a dance associated with the distribution of the wine. The functioning of the objects (vases and musical instruments) is detailed, and shows that one proceeds from the pure wine of the amphoras to the mixture in the krater, to the distribution in pitchers (oinochoai) to consumption from cups and skyphoi.

The large vases are wreathed with ivy, a plant particularly associated with Dionysos. The krater is placed on the earth, a fixed point around which on each face there unfolds a dance performed by six drinkers, each holding a cup.

The musical instruments have complementary functions. The lyre accompanies the player's song, and the flute gives the cadence for the komasts' dance. Everyone, in fact, is dancing, most of them in pairs facing one another, but never parallel. They dance in a group, but each by himself. Under each handle, there is a figure crouched or crawling, heavy with drink.

The komos is shown here as an unruly troupe within a fixed framework, which sets its rules of behavior and its limits.

Satyrs (fig. 171)

An astonishing throng of figures is cleverly arranged around this wine-cooling vase (psykter) designed to be placed inside the krater. Here again the uses of wine are depicted, but in satyric mode: each group suggests an inversion or perversion of human drinking practices.

One satyr displays his virtuosity by balancing a krater on his erect penis, while one of his companions pours him some wine. The same vase with two handles (kantharos) is presented by another satyr: this kind of vase, with its vertical handles, is clearly made for passing from hand to hand. The satyr supports his kantharos, while scarcely touching it.

Around the kantharos, which stands alone and represents Dionysos, two satyrs dance, performing new tricks.

The satyr balanced on his arms, legs in the air, tail hanging down, seems to be responding to the challenge of drinking while upside down without touching the cup, which is placed on the ground like a krater instead of being held as it is supposed to be.

Drinking pure wine, without any human implements, neither krater nor cup, from wineskin to mouth, rejecting any intermediary, the satyr gives himself up to the pure wine. This liquid fire, controlled by Dionysos alone, confers on these hybrid creatures a remarkable ability, allowing them to free themselves from gravity, to go beyond the limits of the human condition, not only in the direction of bestiality, but for a time losing themselves in a supernatural lightness.

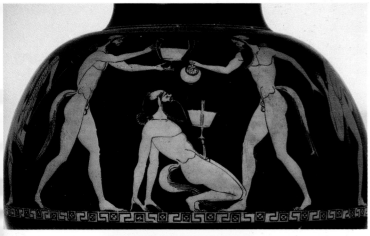

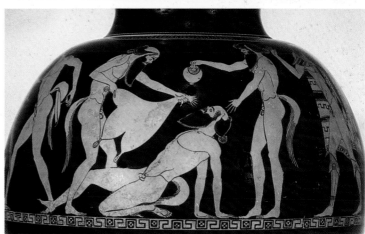

171

127

Correct Use of the Krater (fig. 172 and 173)

The krater by itself defines the mixing and sharing of wine. Its very presence serves to indicate all the values symbolically associated with banquets and drinking parties. Here a young man naked and crowned approaches to dip into the krater, preparing to fill a cup. In the background is an inscription: "Lysis is beautiful," which calls to mind the homosexual eroticism frequently associated with symposia.

Explicitly connected with the symposium by the cup that figures on the reverse, this tondo shows a terracotta jar, half-buried, in which undiluted wine is frequently kept. A satyr dives in, as if to drown himself, leaving only his hindquarters exposed. In this inversion of consumption, it is not the contents of the vase that will fill the belly of the drinker, but the drinker himself who will lose himself in the jar, a belly swallowing up the Dionysiac creature.

172

Of Wine and Women (fig. 174)

The drinking-party (symposium) is a collective experience that gathers the drinkers around wine, music, and women. Luxurious furniture—three couches incrusted with ivory and precious metals—make up a common space in the center of which a flute-girl plays. In front of each couch, there is a table covered with fruit and cakes. Three guests lean on cushions, cups in hand. One sings, his head thrown back; another caresses his partner who unties her hair; the third already embraces his companion. In this masculine environment, the woman has only an instrumental function, whether musical or sexual.

173

On the reverse, the space is organized around the vase—the dinos, a krater placed on a pedestal—in which the wine is mixed. Two slaves carry amphoras whose contents they pour into the larger receptacle, before ladling with the pitchers (oinochoai) placed on the ground. Here again the objects express the stages necessary for the consumption of the wine: storage, transport, mixing, and distribution.

174

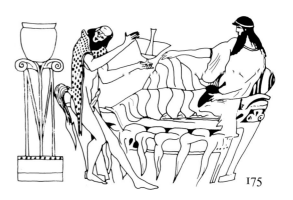

175

Dionysos among us (fig. 175)

Here Dionysos lies alone, self-sufficient. The banquet-space of men appears again in this image, condensed into a picture that juxtaposes the couch and the krater perched high on a tripod. In front of the couch, there is a long table covered with slices of meat. Normally at a sacrifice the gods receive only the fumes from the roasted meats. Here Dionysos, in the same position as the banqueters whose god he is, seems to receive the human portion. In fact, he has in his hand only a bunch of grapes, for him an emblem rather than nourishment.

A satyr playing the role of servant offers him a drinking-cup, the kantharos, a Dionysiac vase that holds only pure wine. Mixed wine, relegated to the left of the picture, holds no interest for the god. In the center of the picture, the kantharos, presented by the satyr, indicates by its proximity to the thyrsos the full force of the pure wine. Finally, the satyr's head, presented frontally, is a supplementary sign of the radical strangeness of the Dionysiac world.

176

177

The Bedmobile (*figs.* 176 *and* 177)

Here Dionysos is reclining, like a banqueter, but on a living couch. It is a strange piece of walking furniture, a he-goat bearded like the god, a familiar animal in Dionysiac processions, which the Greek imagination is quick to associate with satyrs because of its lubricity. This reclining banquet is in a state of movement, as one satyr carries the krater, and the other an enormous skyphos, implements for human use, as opposed to the kantharos, the vessel for pure wine, held by Dionysos. The fixed location becomes a movable feast. On the reverse of the vase, we find Hermes, the god of passages, reclining in the same position, carried by a ram, and accompanied by the god of wine. This image superimposes two complementary and normally separated spaces. In the presence of Dionysos, categories merge and contraries meet.

Crowned by vine-leaves, leaning on an embroidered cushion, this banqueter (fig. 176), isolated within the tondo of the cup on which he is represented, is not alone. A basket hanging in the background evokes the procession of revelers on their way to the symposium. The hare he caresses suggests the young ephebe to whom this love-gift is destined, and whom he would doubtless like to caress in the same way (cf. chap. 5).

His head thrown back, he sings to the strains of music coming from the wings, as one sings at a symposium. An inscription lets us hear the lament accompanying his gesture. It speaks of his love for the young man who is absent: "*O Paidon Kalliste*, o most beautiful of young men…" Here we see the erotic and musical force of poetry conveyed by an image.

For Further Reading

M. Davies, "Sailing, Rowing and Sporting in one's Cups on the Wine-dark Sea," in *Athens Comes of Age. From Solon to Salamis.* Princeton, 1978, 72-90.
J.-M. Dentzer, *Le motif du banquet couché dans le Proche-Orient et le monde grec du VII⁰ au IV⁰ siècle av. J.-C.*, Rome, 1982.
B. Fehr, *Orientalische und griechische Gelage.* Bonn, 1971.
A. Greifenhagen, *Eine attische schwarzfigurige Vasengattung und die Darstellung der Komos im VI. Jahrhundert.* Königsberg, 1929.
F. Lissarrague, *Un flot d'images: une esthétique du banquet grec.* Paris, 1987.

FIG. 178. *Dionysos appears among the hunters; the serving of wine is already shown as a ritual activity.*

FIG. 179. *Dionysos brings together men and women in original choreographies. The norms are transgressed; the women's costumes make the men's nudity stand out even more.*

CHAPTER IX

Satyric Revels

CLAUDE BÉRARD AND
CHRISTIANE BRON

A central figure of the city of images, Dionysos, with his thiasos, is only admitted to the city of men by the stage door. In most Greek cities, the temple of the god adjoined the theater, thus creating a zone shared by religion and spectacle, occupying a space unto itself in the urban fabric. Architecture is insufficient to provide a setting befitting the splendor and power of Dionysos, except through theatrical performances. In the words of Henri Jeanmaire, a scholar with a profound understanding of Dionysos, this god is most often found in movement. The literary sources here agree with the iconographic tradition. Dionysiac festivals first appear as processions leaving the city to spread the festivities throughout the countryside, orchards, and vineyards, as well as on rocky hills and in the forests, the territory of the hunt. The god is really only at home in rocky caves (cf. fig. 30).

Crowned with ivy and holding ivy-sprigs in one hand and the kantharos, his ritual cup, in the other, Dionysos emerges as the grand master of wine in the midst of a group of men, some of whom clearly come from the hunt (fig. 178). Dead hares and foxes hanging by the paws from their sticks attest to the success of the endeavor. The scene is thus situated outside the walls of the city, but that in no way rules out the presence everywhere of wine—in a huge amphora placed in front of the god, in the pitcher with which a young man fills the god's kantharos as if for a libation, in the swollen wineskin carried by a person on the extreme left. We note the singularity of the image. It is not Dionysos who provides drink for the thirsty hunters, but rather the men who serve the god his own invention, the triumphant drink. The level on which the action unfolds is not that of a drinking-bout, the tasting and consumption of a beverage, but rather of a cult. The ivy-branch, held by the hunter on the left, echoes the ones held by the god himself. It points ahead to the recognition signs betokening membership in a thiasos or to the thyrsos, which is more or less equivalent to the Eleusinian initiatory staff (cf. chap. 7, figs. 158 and 160a).

In the second picture (fig. 179), Dionysos is again present, kantharos in hand. Here, however, the effects of his power begin to disrupt the social norms. Not only do the men mingle with the women in a sort of gesticulating dance, but they are also naked. This nudity is all the more striking in its contrast with the richness of

FIG. 180. *The provocative bestiality of the silenoi and satyrs harmonizes with that of the donkey carrying Hephaistos, who has been caught up in the thiasos.*

the women's embroidered costumes. Here we encounter one of the mysterious points of the subversive "disorder" that characterizes the companions of Dionysiac thiasoi.

FIG. 181a. *Is this a humanized satyr* ▷ *or a bestialized man?*

Indeed, in Greece male nudity is not by itself particularly surprising. It was one of the driving elements of Greek art, favoring the search for conformity to an anatomical model whose logical conclusion is the "canon" of Polyclitos, the embodiment of the classical theory according to which beauty expresses the perfect equilibrium between the rhythm and harmony of the proportions only if it simultaneously reflects the highest moral qualities. Here we find that, in an imagery that in other respects multiplies monsters, sirens, gorgons, centaurs (horse-men), pans (men-goats), Dionysos institutes a separate category, that of sileni or satyrs (men-horses). This group enjoys a special status. At times, their animality prevails, and they break out in fits of bestiality. At others, they become human to the point of enacting religious games that manifest sacred forces different from, yet complementary to, those harnessed by the traditional cults of the city (cf. chap. 7, "Festivals and Mysteries").

In origin, these daimons appear to be hybrid creatures made up of a human bust and equine hindquarters (fig. 180). Their nudity reveals legs ending in hooves, and a fine horse's tail grafted to the haunches. Usually in a permanent state of erection, their disproportionate genitals are more like those of a donkey or some other beast, than of a man. Their heads are adorned by two large pointed ears. Their activities revolve around the service of wine, invented by their master Dionysos, music, and dance in which they often engage with maenads, their feminine analogues, with whom they are constantly dallying, without ever being able to calm their sexual frenzy even when they carry them off in their arms. Right off, we see that we are brought to the heart of a system of representations that contrasts with the measured equilibrium and harmony of classical ideals. We are dragged into a sphere ruled by overexcitation of the wildest kind.

FIG. 181b. *The women, maenad-* ▷ *priestesses, carry out the serving of the wine.*

FIG. 182. *Men harvesting.*

FIG. 183. *Satyrs harvesting.*

In the fifth century, however, on a red-figure vase (fig. 181a), a very different sort of satyr approaches a young woman crowned with ivy. He is dressed in a finely pleated long tunic and mantle. Only his animal ears indicate bestiality. The scene is marked by calm, and the relations between the figures show nothing of the original savagery. Yet the thyrsos and ivy testify to the Dionysiac character of the ambiance, a reading confirmed by the other face of the vase (fig. 181b), which shows a maenad, a priestess serving the wine to Dionysos. Thus the satyrs' dress seems to bring them over to the side of the city. They have been tamed, calmed, dressed, civilized—there is no longer anything to distinguish them from the normal citizen apart from the pointed ears which seem more unusual and disturbing here than on the heads of equine monsters. What has happened? What does this difference mean?

To sketch out an answer, we must return to the source, the vine and the wine, over whose preparation Dionysos presides. On this amphora (fig. 182), a large vine-stock is being harvested. Several naked men have climbed the branches and are harvesting the superb bunches. Two baskets are already filled with grapes. We note the stakes that support the branches and form the shoots into a kind of trellis. We do not hesitate to call this a realistic scene, taking into account drawing conventions and technical limitations. The image can be treated ethnographically. It shows us a no longer existing cultural situation and may be compared to analogous harvesting scenes like the beating of olive trees or the gathering of figs. Comparison with the image that follows (fig. 183), however, allows us to observe the action of Dionysiac magic. We see the same vines, the same grape clusters, even the same filled baskets, but tails and ears have transformed the harvesters into satyrs. On the formal level this bestialization of the actors is explained by the presence of Dionysos himself, seated on a folding chair, holding a branch and a kantharos. The god of the vine and master of the satyrs draws the representation towards the supernatural. In contrast to other rural tasks, the harvesting of grapes is here presented as an activity that brings on *enthusiasm*, transforming the existential status of man and placing him in contact with the divine. We note that in many documents the maenads mingle with satyrs, although no women participate in the gathering carried out by the men. We have already seen that the Dionysiac thiasos distin-

134

FIG. 184. *Harvest leads to ritual drinking: Ariadne and Dionysos recline under the arbor.*

FIG. 185. *Vintners trampling the grapes.*

FIG. 186. *Satyrs trampling the grapes.*

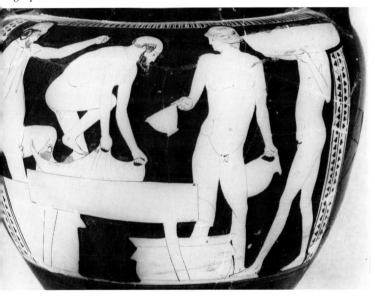

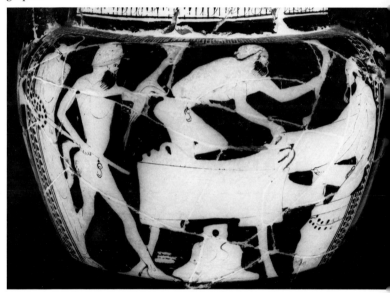

guishes itself from others in being mixed. Satyrs and maenads never remain apart for long and Dionysos himself takes pleasure in female company (fig. 184). Stretched out with Ariadne under the stocks, which form a kind of arbor, the god is depicted according to a pattern suggesting the joyful drinking parties of country festivals. In the Dionysiac sphere, women enjoy a highly privileged status.

At each stage in the preparation of the wine, the same magic comes into play. In one image (fig. 185), the vintners trample the grapes in a sort of strainer with handles placed on the press where the juice flows out. Then, in another, the satyrs take their turn (fig. 186). We have slipped into the Dionysiac world; a satyr holds the thyrsos while a maenad surveys the scene. Wine and vine act as a filter modifying and transcending a seasonal reality. This has little to do with work as such but, through the powers of the sacred beverage, is transformed into a paradisiac activity.

The consumption of wine does not allow the dissipation of ambiguities which arise at each stage of the Dionysiac festival. A cartoon-strip (fig. 187), which runs

FIG. 187a. *A cartoon strip—the banquet.*

FIG. 187b. *The strip continued—the magic of the thiasos.*

FIG. 187c. *The strip continued—men and wine.*

136

along the shoulder of a dinos, juxtaposes scenes illustrating all the levels on which Attic image-makers so skillfully play. Men, gods, heroes, and daimons follow one another in the frieze whose continuity is occasionally broken up by vertical elements. A large symposium brings together several pairs of men leaning on couches; there are low tables laden with food; the dogs chew a bone; a female flute-player entertains the guests. We notice that no one is drinking. However, the cups are hanging on the walls; the wine is not far off. It is perhaps useful to compare this banquet with that of Dionysos and Ariadne (cf. fig. 184). Here (in fig. 187), we are no longer in the god's vineyards but in a room reserved for this purpose. Archaeologists have frequently found ruins of chambers like this with the remains of couches in fixed positions around the room. The wine is thus within the city, but the atmosphere remains secular. On the other hand, if we turn the dinos around and decipher the strip from right to left, we soon fall under the Dionysiac spell (fig. 187b). Dionysos and Ariadne are in the presence of Hephaistos, the blacksmith god who should be returning to Olympos, but is caught here en route, to be initiated into the mysteries of wine. On either side, satyrs and maenads indulge in all kinds of gesticulations. These creatures are of two types. The most bestial correspond to the first category we encountered (cf. fig. 180). The one following Hephaistos' donkey and playing the flute, for example, is more horselike than the two satyrs behind Ariadne. All of them sport triumphant erections, however, which are often emphasized by fillets of consecration. In the right section, unfortunately mutilated, we can make out a maenad dancing between a monstrous satyr and one who is capering, while a third satyr leading an enormous billy-goat is followed by an equine flute-player who has hung his instrument case from his erect penis. In the left hand section, a satyr with a tranquil expression conducts the bull, symbol of the god, to the sacrifice. This is an exceptional detail in this context, emphasizing the effects of the Dionysiac filter functioning here in an episode as "political" as sacrifice (cf. chap. 4, "Sacrificial Slaughter and Initiatory Hunt"). Cups punctuate the space in the field as if to establish a sequence with the banquet hall and to recall the existence of the sacred drink. Finally, even further on the left and without a break in continuity, we encounter purely human actors, whose gestures and postures, however, link them intimately with the satyrs. They are naked, sometimes with an erection. Two of them play the flute like the satyrs while others contort themselves in similar fashion. They wear fillets on their arms (not on their genitals). A man makes advances to an adolescent. Here the presence of the wine is finally made evident—in a colossal krater (like the one carrying this cartoon-strip) over which there hangs a drinking horn and next to which is placed a large cup (no longer hanging from the wall), and in a pitcher depicted in front of the flute-player on the right. Further left, other images show us scenes from heroic mythology depicting sex crimes and the abuses of wine. The frieze is thus composed according to a precise thematic program that reveals exactly where one may engage in the consumption of wine and in sexual excitation while remaining in the Dionysiac sphere. Following this, the painter denounces the excesses and violence of those who do not control their passions.

The large kraters which are the mainstay for serving wine are the perfect surface for Dionysiac imagery. The bellies, shoulders, necks, even the flat part of the upper rim, put before the banqueters' eyes long bands that unroll in a circular fashion, like a circular dance around the vase itself. It is only through technical artifice that we present a horizontal view of this frieze (fig. 188) which was conceived to be read from above. On the original, the continuity of the image favors the establishment of a fusion, without any transition, between humans, daimons, and gods. On either side of the krater and the pitcher placed on the ground, there are men celebrating the power of wine. The dogs recall the banquet context of the preceding scene

(fig. 187a). Immediately, however, we see that the characteristic tails and features of the satyrs signal the irruption of the daimonic. It is worth mentioning once again the important role played by women in this phenomenon. In fact, if one can distinguish a man from a satyr by the bestiality of the latter, no iconographic index allows us to identify the moment of transition from woman to maenad. Our image, moreover, illustrates their perfect homology with satyrs. We have mentioned their active participation in the harvest, and we encounter them here, loaded with full wineskins, pitchers in hand. We notice that a daimon raises his cup in the direction of one of his companions, inciting her to drink, an extremely rare gesture. This is a paradox within the imagery, since the actual consumption of the sacred beverage is almost never shown. Everything takes place on the level of choreographic revels and ritual manipulations. Finally, at the center of the image, the only fixed point, Dionysos is seated, holding a drinking horn in the left hand and a sprig in the right. He receives Hephaistos, mounted on an ithyphallic ass—proof that even a god may enter into the thiasos and benefit from the privilege of Dionysiac joys.

Red-figure compositions show no essential differences. The image on this krater (fig. 189) directly integrates men into the procession of the god (who is not Herakles, as has naively been thought). While Dionysos holds his usual kantharos, the human actors also have their own drinking vessels. Leaning on one another in a posture betraying slight drunkenness, in a state of enthusiasm, they follow with wide steps the hurried gait of Dionysos, preceded by a satyr who seems to be leading them to other celebrations. Here again, a new dimension is introduced into a scene that might have been banal. We may recall the words of the chorus of the *Bacchae* of Euripides (line 409ff.):

> And in the country of beauty,
> Pieria, the home of the Muses,
> the sacred slope of Olympos!
> Take me there, o Bromios, o Roarer!
> leader of the bacchanales! O god of the Evoe!
> There are the Graces and there Desire!
> There the bacchantes have leisure
> to celebrate their holy mysteries.

It is not female bacchants, however, but male ones who progressively reveal this imagery to us.

Letting ourselves be guided by the images, we have put the accent on wine as the main focal point of the thiasos. It would, however, be a mistake to think that the bacchic festival was merely a drunken debauch, or that what we have called Dionysiac magic was simply the result of the heady fumes of the wine. The formal bestiality of the satyrs is not due to an alcoholic vision; the dynamic powers of the festival are to be found elsewhere.

If the goal of these sacred ceremonies is to cause the celebrants to take part in a religious experience that abolishes the distance between them and the divinity—for in this way the human Dionysiac confraternity identifies itself with the eternal mythic confraternity and no longer can Dionysos be distinguished from the priest

FIG. 188. *Another cartoon strip: humans integrated in the Dionysiac dance. Dionysos enthroned receives Hephaistos in the presence of Hermes.*

who embodies him—it is of value for the study of religious phonomena and for an understanding of classical Athenian society to identify the instruments used to attain that goal.

In another ceremonial round-dance (fig. 190), the axis of the composition is a pillar to which is attached a large head of Dionysos—and not a mask of the god. A drapery veils the lower part of the pillar, giving the effigy the form of a mannequin. On the right, a maenad dances, thyrsos in hand, while on the left a satyr, also armed with a thyrsos, dressed in a panther-skin worn crosswise, and strangely shod in short boots, accompanies her to the same rhythm. In relation to the preceding images, the action here unfolds on a different level since the god is no longer present in person, but in the form of a highly artificial idol. Here then we are on the level of cult celebrated by human actors, as is confirmed by the figures on the reverse of the vase running towards the dummy. The continuity of the circle is assured under the handles, on one side by a billy-goat and on the other by a crouching young man, who turns back to call his companions and by a bitch leaping as if to catch the satyr's tail. Exactly what is this satyr doing, with his tail, his erect penis, and his characteristic physiognomy? The sharp contrast between the Dionysiac daimon and the four men running with their dog and goat can be softened by a series of red-figure images that provide a transition. They are of course later chronologically, but we have only to consult the first illustrations in this chapter to see that, taking into account the remarkable stability of Dionysiac phenomena, the ground has been laid for this demonstration from the beginning of our journey through the images. On the reverse side of a krater (fig. 191), two men engage in discussion; nothing distinguishes them from citizens conversing familiarly on other vases except for the thyrsos that stands out in the center of the scene and qualifies its carrier as a faithful follower of the god, a bacchant. In the following image, the thyrsos has disappeared (fig. 192), but one of the interlocutors has the head of a satyr, although nothing evokes the wine or the festival. On another krater (fig. 193), on the other hand, the same satyr follows a woman who turns and with a gesture invites him to join the procession. Bringing up the rear of the procession a torch-bearing woman gives the scene a solemn character while at the same time indicating that the festival probably takes place at night. We notice, then, that the pictorial representations show different stages in the process that gradually transforms citizens into bacchants. It is important to note that Dionysiac magic is not confined to the vineyard, the wine-press, or the territories of the hunt, the forests and caves that are favored places for the cult of Dionysos. It is already manifest in the heart of the city, where even respectable clothing is no obstacle. Of course these satyrs behave in a way that is anything but frenetic. Despite this difference in mood, the symbolic efficacy remains in force. The pointed ear, signaling the Dionysiac world, is still in evidence. Thus the bestiality of satyrs is compatible with the tightly regulated cultural and cultic behaviors in the heart of the city, as we see from the satyr on a skyphos in Chiusi (fig. 181a). The notion of sequence illuminates this phenomenon. The festivals are perhaps spread out over several days. Some episodes take place inside the city. Then the procession gets under way and reaches the area where the more specifically Dionysiac ceremonies may be carried out in complete freedom.

FIG. 190. *The cult celebrated around the effigy of Dionysos brings together satyr, maenad, and bacchants.*

Another red-figure image (fig. 194) allows us to return to the preceding round-dance (cf. fig. 190). We have however progressed in the unfolding of the mysteries—if we understand by mysteries what the Greeks themselves called sacred rites including enthusiasm, vertigo, and trance. On the left of the pillar garlanded with ivy, a maenad plays the flute. On the right, her male homologue in the cultic service holds up towards the mask the ritual cup with vertical handles, the kantharos. We see here a very precise episode and one doubtless charged with holiness, what one could call the "ostension" of the wine on the analogy of the ostension, or showing forth, of the ear of grain in the framework of the mysteries of Eleusis (cf. chap. 7,

FIG. 191. *A bacchant carrying the thrysos.*

FIG. 193. *Departure of the procession for the festival.*

FIG. 189. *Dionysos leads men seduced by the power of wine.*

FIG. 192. *A clothed satyr in conversation with a young man.*

141

FIG. 194. *"Ostension" of the wine by a priest-satyr.*

"Festivals and Mysteries"). The presence of the idol-mannequin, highly artificial and faithfully reproduced by the painter, confirms that we are once again confronted with the activities of a human confraternity. If the maenad by herself is not enough to signal this level, the male acolyte on the other hand is drawn exactly like a mythic satyr, without the accessories of disguise. The contrast between the realism of the improvised idol and the bestialized body of the man playing the satyr indicates a break in the homogeneity of the scene, a gap that brings to light the purpose of the festival. The efficacy of the rites favors the irruption of the daimonic, of enthusiasm, in the literal sense, expressed not in the idol but in those who serve it. The paradoxical encounter between the mask with its very classical profile of the god and the bestial head of the man reveals the profundity of the religious experience. The metamorphosis thus accomplished is the sign of the transcendance and thus of the success of the mysteries just celebrated: man has become satyr.

The mask is the key instrument of this phenomenon. God of the vineyard and of wine, Dionysos is also the god of the mask—of masks, which, let us not forget, had magic as their primary function before they were absorbed into the theatrical framework of spectacle, and which, moreover, have always retained a religious connotation. On a famous krater (fig. 195), one sees a young actor in the process of putting on his costume. He is already got up in some sort of short pants of animal skin to which are affixed a fake tail and phallus, and in his left hand he holds the mask of the satyr whose role he will play. Thus we are in the world of theatrical representation—more precisely, we are peeking into the wings to see the actors' preparations. On the right, on the other hand, we are in the presence of a real satyr. We have changed levels, without any transition, and we are in the divine sphere of Dionysos. The image, in a juxtaposition made more striking by photographic cutting, places the human actor and his mythological model face to face. But we must push this analysis further and attempt to put the two figures into closer relation. On the level of the imagery, the scene on the right could also represent the performance of the play being prepared on the left. Accomplishing their full function, the elements of disguise would transform their wearer and would instantly lose their artificial character, becoming invisible. The spectacle as a whole would tilt toward

142

the Dionysiac world it is supposed to represent. By virtue of his costume, the young actor would become, in the heat of the action, a real satyr—note the vegetal garland transferred from his hair to the bald forehead of the satyr. In this way, a greater understanding of theatrical workings allows us to take account of an aspect of the Dionysiac mysteries.

By analyzing the role of the mask, we are able to define the problem of the figurative realism of the imagery. It must be noted that the mask is in effect only represented when it is not being worn (fig. 195) and not concealing the features of the face. This crucial observation holds true as much for the actors as for the satyrs and bacchants. Once it is put on, its artificial character disappears and its wearer, by virtue of its symbolic effect, becomes that which he impersonates, a satyr. Even in images with explicit reference to the theatrical world, in the framework of the satyr-play performed after the trilogy of classical tragedies, the mask cannot be identified.

FIG. 195. *A game of masks: the theatrical creation of a satyr.*

FIG. 196. *Costume with appendages: the ritual creation of a satyr.*

This phenomenon is all the more surprising, since the second element of the disguise, the shorts with a horse tail and a pointed penis, is not systematically made to disappear. Some images (fig. 196) put onstage satyrs whose heads appear relatively natural by comparison with the genitals and tail clearly presented as artificial attributes. Such documents verify the existence of elements of costume in the mysteries of Dionysos and in non-theatrical contexts. In another image (fig. 197), the satyr faces a maenad with a thyrsos and an animal skin worn crosswise. Brandishing a drinking horn, he exhibits a fake phallus attached to a pair of short furry pants—the centerpiece of his costume—to which is also attached a tail whose tip can be seen waving behind him. That this costume has nothing to do with the theater is shown unambiguously by a vase with a woman disguised as a satyr (fig. 198). 143

FIG. 197. *A man dressed as a satyr and a woman disguised as a maenad.*

FIG. 198. *Costume with appendages: the creation of a female satyr.*

FIG. 199. *A man and a woman await the beginning of the ceremonies; only the thyrsos signals the proximity of Dionysos.*

FIG. 201. *The priestly function of the maenads.*

We note that women do not undergo equine metamorphosis. Bestial monstrosity, at least in the Dionysiac context, has no hold on the feminine body, despite the satyr's shorts and fake phallus (which do, however, raise other questions). This extraordinary disguise requires nudity and differentiates women from maenads. They never have animal ears since they do not wear masks: we have already seen that it is the mask and not the shorts that sets in motion the transformation. On the contrary, the feminine delicacy of their features contrasts sharply with the faces of the satyrs. When they wear the satyr's short pants, their naked breasts emphasize the incongruity of the male member grafted to their lower half. These women who play the satyr in a solitary dance, properly satyric, often around a kantharos filled with wine, contrast with the dressed maenads, armed with the thyrsos and always in a group, the companions of satyrs, Dionysiac priestesses by turns solemn or out of control. The intensity and diversity vary greatly at different moments of the festival and the satyric games do not always provoke the same reactions. One of the leitmotifs of Dionysiac ceremonies surfaces here again: strange relations are established between the sexes, upsetting all the norms of the city.

The intensity of the religious experience is not expressed in the same way for a woman as for a man. She is sometimes disguised as a satyr, but the artifice always remains evident; she never becomes a real satyr. We can however discover the effect of Dionysiac magic on women through modifications of costume and gesture.

Thus on the tondo of a cup (fig. 199), a man and woman are brought together. Only the thyrsos indicates the relation to Dionysos, without the festival being signaled by wine, music, or dance. We are at a preparatory stage as in figures 191 and

FIG. 200a. *The initiation of a maenad: satyric music.*

FIG. 200b. *The initiation of a maenad: satyric dance.*

FIG. 200c. *The maenad enters the dance and brandishes the Dionysiac insignia.*

192. The pose of the woman, entirely wrapped in a mantle that leaves only her head bare, is remarkable: she seems to be waiting for something; no gesture links her to her companion. A cup in Oxford (fig. 200), which reproduces various moments of what we will call the "initiation" of a maenad, furnishes us with the elucidation of this scene. On the central tondo (fig. 200a), in the posture we have just observed, a woman watches a satyr standing in front of her. He plays the flute and seems to invite his companion to be drawn in by the enchanting music. There remains no trace of disguise on the officiant of Dionysos: the tail and ears suggest a mythic satyr, and yet we are certain of the human level of this rite. Corresponding to

145

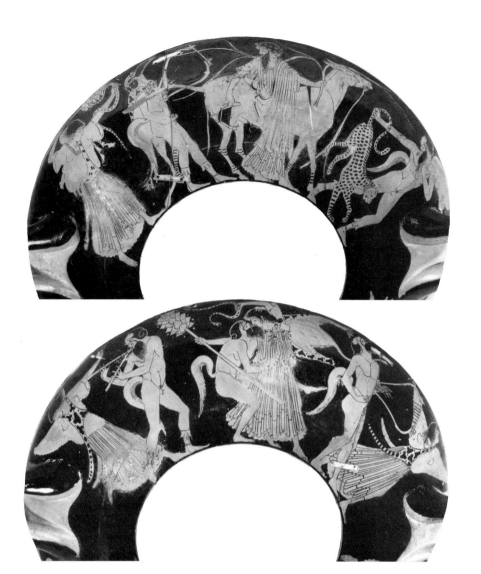

FIG. 202a. *The thiasos on the loose: music, snakes, wild animals.*

FIG. 202b. *The thiasos on the loose: ecstatic and erotic dances.*

the substitution of the young man by a satyr, there is a very slight modification in the posture of the future maenad. Her left arm is slightly folded, which prevents her thyrsos from slipping without its being held. In the following stage (fig. 200b), the woman is seated in the same position but two satyrs surround her; they dance around her, stroking her with their hands, seeking by the excitation of the dance rhythm to provoke the Dionysiac enthusiasm. The thyrsos is not yet taken in the hand, which remains hidden under the cloak, but it is now held upright. On the second face of the cup (fig. 200c) the woman has thrown off her cloak. Dressed in the nebris, she brandishes the Dionysiac insignia. Her entry into the satyrs' dance associates her by now with the thiasos: she has become a maenad. Just as one can follow the creation of a satyr, one can also, from image to image, watch the subtle transformation of existential status of the woman who gradually becomes identified with the maenads of the mythic thiasos.

 The roles of maenads are as varied as those of satyrs. The sequence of the festival is composed of an alternation of "strong" and "weak" moments, solemn phases and sudden outbursts. No other ceremony in ancient Greece is so marked by violent rhythmic constrats. Calm and collected, the Dionysiac priestesses not only serve wine to their god, but they also crown him with a garland of ivy as if in an act of consecration (fig. 201). A truly pious image, the scene reflects as much as imposes the appropriate and efficacious behaviors that are easily inscribed in the repertoire of fundamental acts of Greek religion. But then the thiasos begins to move and reaches the forests and their secret grottoes. Following the god, satyrs and maenads, both equally possessed, throw themselves into a frenzied dance, brandishing snakes and playing with wild animals (fig. 202a). The wailing of satyric flutes sets the maenads to whirling like dervishes. The satyrs become intoxicated by their own music and, in their contagious excitement, do not hesitate to approach their companions more intimately (fig. 202b). The great drums mingle their hollow tonalities of exotic gongs with the sounds of the wind and stringed instruments (fig. 203). Heads thrown back express the degree of the ecstatic trance attained by the participants. The flaps of clothing fly open. The women spin around, their clothing coming undone. And yet, on one side, Dionysos and Ariadne sit calmly, looking into each other's eyes, while, on the other, a bacchant rejoins the dancers, carrying a small child on her shoulders!

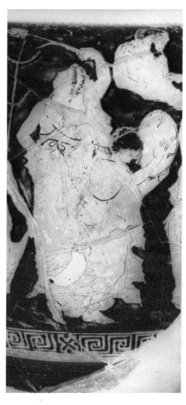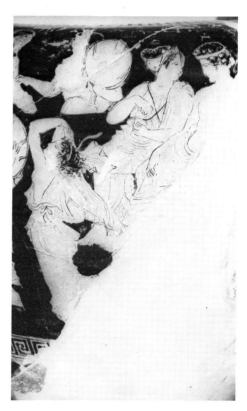

FIG. 203. *Disheveled maenads whirl around to the sound of gongs.*

In this teeming imagery, the surprises multiply. When the dance achieves its paroxysm, the maenads give themselves up to *omophagia* and *diasparagmos*, tearing apart and eating raw the wild animals they have captured (fig. 204). These practices, attested by ethnologists, are only conceivable in a state of mystic hysteria, the consequence and end-result of the linked effects of music and dance.

Dionysos himself participates in the most exacerbated violence. He incarnates all the ambiguities and the frenzies of the magic sphere which he animates by his mere presence. On the one hand, his long black beard emphasizes his virility, and on the other, his feminine garments recall the strange shifts in gender effected by

147

FIG. 204. *The* diasparagmos, *ritual dismemberment of animals.*

◁ FIG. 205. *The prince of maenads and satyrs in the paroxysm of the ecstatic crisis.*

cross-dressing (fig. 205). If women can play at being satyrs, satyrs can also disguise themselves as maenads. Dionysos is the prince of maenads. In the face of this troubling silhouette in which the transparent skirt and finely pleated blouse billowing over the belt are combined with the skin of some spotted cat, before this maddened gesticulation and these hands clenched around the paws of the fawn torn apart by supernatural force, emptied of blood, we understand the sacred horror that seized the Greeks. God or priest, myth or reality, the question is no longer relevant. The imagery is precisely the place where all the contradictions of our fantasmagoric imaginings are resolved.

For Further Reading

C. Bron, "Porteurs du thyrse ou bacchants" in *Images et société en Grèce ancienne: L'iconographie comme méthode d'analyse.* Lausanne, 1987, 145-154.

C. Caruso, "Travestissements dionysiaques" in *Images et société en Grèce ancienne,* 103-110.

M. Detienne, *Dionysos Slain.* Baltimore, 1979 (translation by Mireille and Leonard Muellner of *Dionysos mis à mort,* Paris, 1977).

H. Jeanmaire, *Dionysos, histoire du culte de Bacchus.* Paris, 1978 (1951).

K. Kerényi, *Dionysos: Archetypal Image of Indestructible Life.* London, 1976.

W. F. Otto, *Dionysos, Myth and Cult.* Bloomington, 1965 (translation by Robert B. Palmer of *Dionysos: Mythus und Kultus,* Frankfurt, 1933, 2nd ed. 1948).

CHAPTER X

In the Mirror of the Mask

FRANÇOISE FRONTISI-DUCROUX

FIG. 206. *Dionysos, in human form, living and familiar, in the company of a satyr.*

FIG. 207. *His rigid idol—a pillar surmounted by a mask and enveloped by a flowing garment—is surrounded by a ring of wild maenads.*

When the vase, even as it presents itself to be looked at—offering the banqueter selected representations of the city, its activities, and its models—begins to look back at the drinker, to fix his eyes with its own, the serene relationship of the spectator to the image becomes troubled, and the one-way relation of subject to object is inverted. It is especially in the sphere of Dionysos that this confusion takes place—indeed, this is the function of the god.

Although representations of Dionysos exhibit great variety, they do not by any means exhaust the possibilities of metamorphosis that the myths attribute to him, relating, for example, that he loves to show himself in the form of a bull or a snake. But in the context of Attic pottery alone, he, more than any other god, is shown in a multiplicity of different forms. Like the other Olympians, he appears full-length, animated, provided with an anthropomorphic body and designated by specific attributes. But the same features that identify him unmistakably—the long robe and crown of ivy—could also be hung from a rigid pole surmounted by a mask. And the mask alone, bearded and crowned, is often shown head on, taking up all or part of the image.

A cup in the Berlin Museum (fig. 206) brings together the first two of these manifestations. At the bottom of the empty vessel, or through the reflections of the liquid, the tondo reveals the familiar and physical presence of the god attentive to the sound of the flute played by a satyr whom he regards fixedly. Around its outer circumference (fig. 207), the idol is surrounded by an undulating circle of maenads unleashed by the exultation of the dance, which takes its rhythm from another flute. But the profile of the mask is turned away from the musician, and its glance passes indifferently over the agitated heads. The showy garment, sumptuously embroidered, falls in vertical pleats modeled over a void, draping an absent body. Despite the similarity of its features, the beard and the hair falling in ringlets to the shoulders, this rigid armless idol with its oriental appearance contrasts in every respect with the supple and mobile figure on the tondo whose more sober clothing falls in voluptuous curves suggesting a living presence.

It is paradoxically in his own world, wild and divine, in the bestial proximity of his companions, that the god makes himself most human. In the world of men who 151

call on him, invoke him, and seek through ritual to establish him among them, between the altar where they offer him sacrifices and the krater where, according to his law, they mix the wine, Dionysos remains far off, distant in the presence of his effigy, as if a stranger to the animation of the women whom he inspires and subjugates to his possession. It is in them that he is to be found, as much as in the krater crowned with ivy, much more than in his impenetrable appearance.

This tension between presence and absence is brusquely abolished on a cup in the museum of Boulogne. The god is there (fig. 208), head on, seated, between two giant eyes that duplicate the wide-eyed and easy-going look with which he regards the spectator. His entire body is shown, framed by a throne, in a sort of face that covers the side of the cup. He offers himself, lucid and smiling, in the benevolence of the wine whose consumption is a direct communion between the god and the drinker, his celebrant. The Vlasto oinochoe (fig. 209) brings us back to the world of ritual and reestablishes the distance with an image that is pure spectacle. Between two women with reverential postures who carry the sacred accessories, the great mask, seen in profile, is laid on a basket, the liknon, a place often occupied by the phallic symbol or the god himself as a newborn. This substitution affirms the strangeness of the cult and its specificity.

On an oinochoe in Berlin (fig. 210), the mask is in place, propped on a pillar, but gigantic—it takes up almost the entire height from base to capital. Lacking a body, it is only a face, enigmatic and fascinating. To its right, a woman in the posture of a maenad seems to back away. But her arm, tipping a pitcher of wine towards the god

FIG. 208. *Seated facing forward, enigmatic, the enthroned god, between two giant eyes.*

FIG. 210. *The mask of the god, against a column; on the right, a woman holds a pitcher of wine.*

FIG. 209. *The bearded and crowned mask, laid in a ritual basket, receives honors and offerings.*

as if for a libation, and her profile turned towards him bring us back again to that great face and that unavoidable gaze. The distinguishing characteristic of the mask would seem to be its frontality. Yet, as we have seen in one example, it can be portrayed in profile, as are the faces of both gods and men traditionally, objectified like them into pure representation. But on the cup in Berlin, this figurative positioning indicates above all the god's retreat and distance at the very moment when his presence is most powerful.

A lekythos in New York (fig. 211) offers another solution. A very large mask, suspended from a pillar, is duplicated, showing two profiles tied back to back, two beards, and two eyes. In this way the two glances diverge, encompassing the narrow circumference of the vase, covering in two directions the space where the women dance and salute the idol. This procedure projects the image of the pillar encircled by the round-dance onto a cylindrical surface and suggests the dancers' effort to circumscribe the divine power by their circular movement. The image also evokes the

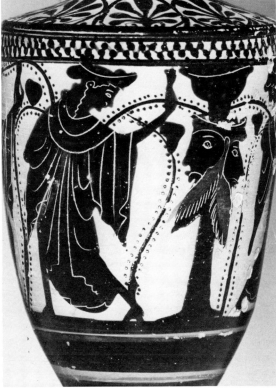

FIG. 211. *Women dance all around the pillar. The redoubling of the mask suggests the revolving circle which surrounds it.*

god's presence, granted in return, the fullness of his glance, and his ubiquity. He is presented as the one who sees all.

On another lekythos, in Palermo (fig. 212), the mask is shown frontally. Enormous, its height takes up all of the figural surface, and eyes are fixed on the spectator, head-on. From its open mouth—an exceptional feature—there seems to issue a loud cry. All around, a celebration seems to be in preparation. Four figures, two satyrs and two maenads, leap, brandishing thyrsos, snake, and cup. This evocation of the god's wild environment is framed by two columns defining the architecture— a sanctuary, a constructed space. This contrast adds its effect to the fundamental disproportion between the giant head, propped on its beard and the ends of its 153

FIG. 212. *On either side of the wide-eyed and open-mouthed divine face, satyrs and maenads leap in the exaltation of the trance.*

curls, and the minuscule figures moving around it. Each of the maenads leaps across, or over, the back of a satyr, in a prodigious jump suggesting the breaking of the bonds of gravity, the flight made possible by the supernatural force liberated by the trance. Their acrobatic leaps carry them outside the field reserved for the image, their heads encroaching on the upper border. This transgression of the figural space, this escape upwards, elevates the women above the customary companions of the god—half-men, half-beasts—transporting them beyond human and social limits. All these techniques vie to produce a graphic equivalent of the disorganization and liberation characteristic of Dionysiac activity.

The motif of the large "prophylactic" eyes is most frequent on drinking cups and amphoras. Is it protection against the ill effects of the drink they contain and against evil spirits watching over the drinker's shoulder to cast the evil eye on him? Or is it a reminder of the indispensable social control presiding over banquets and drinking parties, sometimes by the intermediary of monitors called *Ophthalmoi*,

FIG. 213. *On the sides of cups the staring face of Dionysos rivets the drinker even while protecting him.*

FIG. 214. *The god of wine watches ▷ from the bellies of his amphoras.*

FIG. 215. *Through the reflections of the wine, at the bottom of the cup, there appears the grimacing face of a satyr representing the bestiality that wine can bring out in everyone.*

the eyes. But when it is the face of Dionysos with its haunting expression that is inscribed (fig. 213), there is no longer any question of self-control or precaution. One must succumb to the ascendency of the god. In the mask watching from the side of an amphora (fig. 214) like the mask the banqueter brings up to his own face, the wine itself is visualized, even as it is about to be drunk, in the glow of the divine liquid—the god himself. The confrontation between the drinker and Dionysos, across the raised cup, creates an almost initiatory connection, a mirror-game in which the god flashes a reflection of his divinity towards the man—as in the ambiguous speech in the *Bacchae* of Euripides, in which Dionysos, pretending to be merely one of his own followers, tells Pentheus of his initiation into the mysteries: "I saw the god see me."

"Wine is the mirror of the soul" the poets and philosophers never tire of repeating. When the mirror of the cups presents the wild face of a satyr (fig. 215) to the Athenian citizen, what truth does it reveal to him? The joyful exuberance, the frolics, the hilarity of the companions of Dionysos certainly express the liberating madness that imposes itself on whoever receives the god and throws into question, with him, the categories of the organized world, breaking down the barriers sepa rating animal from man, man from god, obliterating social roles, sex, and age. But when a bestial and hairy face with horse's ears turns toward the spectator and with its widened eyes looks deeply into his own, the confrontation can only be disquieting. The drinker who finds a necessary experience of alterity in the wine also discovers in himself his least divine part, sees the awakening of the animality nestled in the heart of the civilized. The satyr who often serves as a (negative?) example of the transgressive use of wine, intruding with an anomalous sexuality, presents man with the image of his hidden desires, of the savagery he holds in check, the exhibition of a truth quite different from his official identity.

There is a divine power that only functions by means of the mask, expressing itself only in frontal representations. This is Gorgo, a monstrous winged female creature who, even when represented standing, before her decapitation by Perseus, turns her flat, distended, wide-eyed face (fig. 216) toward the spectator.

Frontality is so much a part of her personality that a painter has tried, on the inside of a strange cup in Copenhagen (fig. 217), to compensate by duplication for the laterality of her body, necessary at least for the representation of the legs. Thus both sides of Gorgo are seen at the same time. Below, four legs, bent to indicate running, face each other two by two. The two profiles are simplified above, resolving into one arm on each side, and a third hand in the middle. The two bodies support a single head and an enormous, swollen face.

The story of the gorgon is well known. Perseus, in order to kill Medusa, the only mortal one of the three sisters, without succumbing to her deathdealing glance, turns and cuts her throat, guiding his arm by the reflection in the bronze shield of Athena. He hides the hideous head in his sack, pulling it out in times of need to turn his enemies to stone. For, although dead, Medusa continues to bring death. He then brings the head to Athena, who places it in the center of her aegis, using it to arouse an irrepressible panic in the armies of men. Similarly, the epic warrior wears the gorgoneion on his shield as an emblem to frighten the enemy. And, in the heat of battle, it is the same glance of the gorgon that shines in the eyes of the hero in fury, and it is her grimacing face that appears on his distorted features. It is thus the irresistible incarnation of death whose approach chills the most tempered hearts and paralyzes the limbs.

Gorgo, the power of the beyond, also lives at the border of the world of the Dead. Odysseus, the all-enduring hero, hesitates at the entrance to Hades—"Green

FIG. 216. *After having decapitated the gorgon, Perseus flees, pursued by the monster's sisters.*

fear seized me that the noble Persephone would send the gorgon head of this terrifying monster from the depths of Hades." If he were to continue along his way, he knows he would be transformed like Gorgo, and under her glance become like the dead who are mere heads—empty, without force—"heads enveloped in night."

The mask of Gorgo, by its monstrosity, renders visible to humans the radical otherness of night, which blurs and mixes categories distinguished by the world of the living. The bestial mingles with the human: a leonine muzzle, enormous bovine ears, an animal mane, often bristling with snakes. The mouth slit in a rictus discloses the fangs of a wild beast and the tusks of a boar. The tongue, sticking out, hangs down covering the chin. Thus the masculine is superimposed on the femi- 157

FIG. 217. *Two bodies for one head— or two sides of the mask?*

FIG. 219. *The monster as a caricature of itself.*

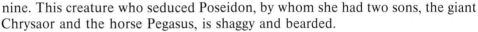

FIG. 218. *Gorgo is everywhere, sticking out her tongue.*

nine. This creature who seduced Poseidon, by whom she had two sons, the giant Chrysaor and the horse Pegasus, is shaggy and bearded.

To this horrifying vision is added an aural dimension emphasized by the literary texts. No articulate voice, however, issues from the gorgon's distended mouth. There are instead indistinct gurgles, the grinding of teeth, the gnashing of jaws, all dominated by the hissing of snakes. It was to imitate these piercing cries that Athena invented the flute. But while playing, she saw mirrored in a fountain her puffed out, deformed cheeks, the gorgon face. Disgusted, she threw down her new toy and the satyr Marsyas made off with it. Ever since, the flute, which leads warriors to battle and to death, which arouses dancing and inspires trance, can also be the instrument of delirium, madness, and the crisis of possession. In the face of the possessed—eyes rolled back, features contorted, tongue darting, teeth grinding—we see the face of the gorgon emerging once again.

The texts are explicit on the meaning of Gorgo: she is absolute horror, the incarnation of the most frightening aspects of the supernatural, the shadows, and the void of death. The question arises, then, why this multiplication of images of something defined as intolerable, the forbidden vision, the glance that must be avoided at all costs? For Gorgo is everywhere, on temple pediments, in craftsmens' workshops, in private houses, infinitely repeated on furniture, utensils, and vases (fig. 218). Here again, her role is apotropaic. She keeps away malevolent powers, turning the menace into protection, inverting her own maleficent power, for the benefit of the owner of the object that carries her effigy, turning it against potential enemies. This is the first explanation. But, as with the masks of Dionysos and of the satyrs who alternate with him on the bellies of vases and at the bottom of cups, its function is also to exorcise the interior demons, the fears, the anguish, the terror before the definitive alterity of death, all that which in the world of the living can only be evoked in words, and which will only be seen in the silence of the beyond. The mask of the Gorgon presents to humans, as the bronze mirror of the shield to Perseus, an attenuated, bearable reflection of that "invisible." It is more bearable because the figural representation often chooses, unlike the texts, to accentuate the grotesque side of ugliness, and since these images, although they do not totally obscure the hidden menace, are laughable, playful, often funny, as we see from an

159

astonishing gorgoneion on a hydria in London (fig. 219). Surrounded by a ring of snakes cleverly arranged in rhythmic undulations, under her carefully curled hair, between an array of teeth provided with regulation fangs, Gorgo diligently shows off a square tongue. And to make her sex clear, this bogey-woman coquettishly wears a pair of earrings. This is an extreme case. But virtually all representations of the Gorgon's mask exploit in this way the essential ambivalence of the grimace that alternately arouses fear and laughter, thus providing the Greeks in their daily life with the visible manifestation of a horror that has been tamed.

The human face can also establish a reciprocity of the glance, brought about by the full-face encounter between the mask and the one looking at it. When one of these figures, escaping the convention of the profile, presents itself full-face, the

FIG. 220. *The falling warrior, shown frontally, already wears the mask of death on his face.*

FIG. 221. *Like the dying man, the sleeper presents his face head on. Hypnos, the spirit of sleep, has come to settle on the body of the giant Alkyoneus.*

spectator feels implicated in this confrontation in quite another way than when he encounters a supernatural presence. But this occurs only in precise contexts and as an exception, since even in these contexts, representation in profile remains the rule.

The motif of the glorious death of the warrior constitutes the model of excellence for the Greek citizen. Thus these scenes of combat furnish a frequent theme for the decoration of vases. Sometimes a warrior dying under the blows of the enemy is shown full face and offers up for view a face marked by the proximity of death: wild eyes, clenched jaw, features calling to mind the beyond. On a cup with eyes, the central position is occupied by a warrior presented in almost complete frontality (fig. 220). Bending, he places one knee on the ground and sways backwards, completely exposing the inside of his shield and his unprotected body. The bowed head is hidden under the helmet, whose oval shape allows only the tip of the beard to show. This strange form is broken up only by the vertical lines of the nosepiece and by the design of the eye-holes, which encircle and emphasize the wavering eyes. The total effect is of a terrifying mortuary mask, inhuman, a negation of the face, which already belongs to the invisible beyond. The two large eyes of the cup repeat, in their sinuous outline, the eyes of the dying man—the focal point of

FIG. 222. *An exhausted Persian sleeps. The bow hung above him seems to indicate the fatigue of battle, but the drinking horn below suggests drunkenness.*

FIG. 223. *At the moment of greatest effort, the wrestler turns his partly masked face towards the spectator.*

the composition—eyes of the hero who looks death in the face and throws a last glance at the world of men. The frontality expresses in striking fashion this liminal position and perhaps also the tragic ambivalence of the glorious death that removes the warrior from humanity.

Thanatos, the divinity of death, has, for the Greeks, a twin brother, Hypnos, sleep. In epic, they are shown together lifting up their favored heroes from the battlefield. Because of their kinship, and because Hypnos also opens up the way to another world where, in dreams, man can enter into contact with the gods and the dead, the sleeper is sometimes represented full-face on vases. The theme of the sleeping maenad, exhausted by her wanderings and by running after the god, and vulnerable, while resting, to the lust of the satyrs, may be treated frontally, as we see on a cup in the Louvre (G 251). It is the same for another mythic sleeper, the giant Alkyoneus, who, stretched out on his mother earth, smiles from time to time while dreaming, as his murderer Herakles approaches. A winged genius sits on or passes over his sprawling body. This is Hypnos, whose presence is thus doubly marked (fig. 221). In banquet scenes, where the motif of sleep intertwines with that of drunkenness, one may find, under a cup handle, a small slave asleep, seated facing out. Another cup shows, in its tondo, an exhausted and happy Persian; at his feet, the rhyton (drinking horn) denotes the use of unmixed wine, normal for a barbarian (fig. 222). These faces with closed eyes suggest at the same time the exploration of one of the borders of human existence, and the escape, the loss of consciousness that characterizes sleep.

A third context is furnished by the scenes of battle and great physical effort. In the framework of the gymnasium, when two wrestlers come to grips, one of the two always turns his face toward the spectator (fig. 223). It is sometimes the victor, at the moment of greatest effort, and sometimes the vanquished, almost paralyzed and annihilated by his adversary's hold. The face presented is often half-hidden by a hand grabbing it or arms choking it.

On a vase in the Villa Giulia (fig. 224), Herakles, in a similar position, holds Nereus, the old man of the sea. The hero grips the god in his powerful arms, trying

161

FIG. 224. *Herakles conquers Nereus, the old man of the sea, master of metamorphosis. His triumphant face emerges from the maw of the Nemean lion, whose skin he wears.*

by encircling him to put an end to his metamorphoses. Herakles' face, which shows intense effort, strangely seems to issue from the mouth of the lion whose skin he wears. The superhuman character of the hero and this feat, emphasized by the full-face presentation, is in this way marked by animality and savagery.

Another situation susceptible to frontal treatment is the playing of the flutist. On the François vase (fig. 225), among the hundred-odd figures represented, the only ones presented head on, aside from the Gorgon under each handle, are Dionysos, who fixes his penetrating eyes upon all comers, and the muse Kalliope. For the muse, the frontality which extends to her entire body is not due to a particularity of her divine status, but to the Pan-pipes (syrinx) with which she accompanies the nuptial procession of Thetis and Peleus. When the flute-player is a satyr, the frontality is probably overdetermined. But when it is a flute-player at a symposium

FIG. 225. *On the François vase, in the long parade of gods and goddesses, only Dionysos and the muse Kalliope, who plays the flute, are shown frontally.*

FIG. 226. *Total frontality, almost excessive, for this flute-playing satyr.*

FIG. 227. *At a human banquet, the flute-player reproduces the high-pitched cries of the gorgon and his puffed-out cheeks recall her distended mask.*

FIG. 228. *The head of the drinker sinking into drunkeness barely emerges from the cup which partly masks it.*

(fig. 227), the painter's choice arises only from the specific characteristics of the flute. A necessary accessory of the Dionysiac trance and the human consumption of wine, its invention is linked, as we have seen, to the figure of the Gorgon. Its sharp sounds are believed to imitate the monster's inarticulate cries, and the puffed-out cheeks of the musician also reproduce its swollen mask. This initial association is strengthened by what we learn from the texts on the connection of flute-music to delirium, madness, and possession. The flute appears as the musical dimension of the mask, its equivalent in sound. It provokes aurally the same effect that results visually from the meeting of a human and a divine glance: an opening to alterity, a break in the daily routine caused by a sudden eruption of otherness. It is this correspondence that is suggested by the mute image of the flute-player who plays facing outwards, his eyes turned towards ours.

Ultimately it is his own face that the drinker encounters while looking into the cup he brings to his lips. It is a double of himself, the reflection of his drunkenness, sinking into the skyphos, only the lost eyes emerging from the vessel (fig. 228). But the vase as mirror can also send back to him the ironic image of the excesses of drinking and their discomforts, the illness, vertigo, and nausea, as we see from the banqueter who shows his anxious face as he vomits, supported by a young slave.

Through masks whose stares force the drinker to face supernatural powers, and human faces in which he sees reflected various possible versions of himself, the frontal representation of the vases suggests a visual exploration of the frontiers of the human condition, of the maximum difference of the divine, of bestiality or of the beyond, of certain forms of an otherness internal to humanity. In these situations man reaches his own limits, escaping from himself by surpassing or annihilating them. The graphic choices emphasize the continuity of this process. The tension between presence and absence, proximity and distance, which the mask expresses conventionally in the fixity of its empty eyes or by the mismatch of its features, is found again in most of the frontal representations which, for one reason or another, are rarely shown in their entirety. There is the head of the fallen warrior hidden under his helmet, the closed eyes of the sleeper and sometimes of the dying man, the partially hidden features of the flutist playing, of the winning fighter, or of the drinker losing consciousness, faces that at the same time offer and withhold themselves—partly hidden, half-masked—images simultaneously of similarity and difference.

The symbolic value of the glance can be made more explicit, almost material, by the image. The large prophylactic eyes on cups and amphoras are composed—as are the eyes of masks—of a series of concentric circles, the black disc in the center taken as an especially dilated pupil. Thus a cup in Cambridge (fig. 230) shows, surrounded by a first circle (the iris), a perfectly circular and complete gorgoneion, with the mouth open in a wide slit, the tongue stuck out, and once again, large eyes open wide. Here the monstrous face occupies the place of the pupil, whose Greek name *kore*, means "young girl," just as does the Latin word *pupilla*. Plato explains that to see oneself one must look into the eyes of another, and that there one can see oneself in the tiny silhouette reflected in the center of the eye. In the center of each eye, repeated twice on each of its faces, this cup shows, in place of the "young girl," the petrifying head of Gorgo, the very one brandished by that other Kore, the queen of the Underworld, Persephone, at the threshold of her kingdom. The drinker who looks into these giant eyes contemplates there his final truth, the face of his own death.

Masks are mute. The mask rigorously exploits the logic of this quality of muteness proper to the image. It expresses what it has to say to men in the silence of its glances and by resonances radically opposed to articulated language: the strange lowing of rhombes in the Dionysiac cult, the satyrs' inhuman groans, the piercing

163

yelps of gorgons in mythic tales, and always and everywhere, the disturbing sound of the flute, whose music, incompatible with the voice and singing, has the function of evoking all that cannot be said. Similarly, the liminal situations where the human face is represented full-face are also those in which man remains without a voice, losing the use of language, having, at best, recourse to a cry in the instant of death, during sleep and in drunkenness, at the moment of supreme effort, and of course when his mouth is blocked by the flute he is playing.

These speechless vases, which never cease telling their users of the lives of men and gods, the city, war and death, tell also of their own silence and of the specificity of their language. In becoming anthropomorphized, they may become only a head, may take on only a face, like the fascinating "living" cup in the British Museum (fig. 231). Its shape gives it the name *mastos*, breast. Between the two ears of the handles, two large expressive eyes frame the shape of a nose. But below, there is no mouth. What could better indicate than this absence the mute eloquence of the image, signifying the particular character, irreducible to any other, of figurative language.

FIG. 229. *The banqueter encounters at the bottom of the vase an ironic image of the excesses of drinking.*

FIG. 230. *In the center of the apotropaic eyes, the pupils have the face of Gorgo—protection for the drinker who buries his face in the cup or an image of inescapable death?*

FIG. 231. *The vase becomes a face, ▷ but there is no mouth, because it speaks in silence.*

For Further Reading

ON THE MASK:

B. Freyer-Schauenburg, "Gorgoneion skyphoi." *JdI* 85, 1970, 1-27.
F. Frontisi-Ducroux and J.-P. Vernant, "Figures du masque en Grèce ancienne." *Journal de Psychologie*, 1983, 53-69.
W. Wrede, "Der Maskengott." *Ath. Mitt.* 53, 1928, 66-95.

ON THE GORGON:

H. Besig, *Gorgo und Gorgoneion in der archaischen griechischen Kunst.* Berlin, 1937.
K. Schauenburg, *Perseus in der Kunst des Altertums.* Bonn, 1960.
J.-P. Vernant, *La Mort dans les yeux: figures de l'autre en Grèce ancienne.* Paris, 1986.

ON FRONTALITY:

F. Frontisi-Ducroux, "La Mort en face", *Metis* 1, 2, 1986, 197-213.

Postscript

CLAUDE BÉRARD

Entering the imagery is perhaps easier than leaving it. Despite the many images we have presented, the journey is unfinished and will always remain so. Simply from the practical point of view, it is in fact impossible to display simultaneously all the scenes necessary to close the circle. We may even ask ourselves whether such a project would be worthwhile, given a system of representation which, in the final analysis, exists only in the imagination of each of us. We have rather set out to describe the specific character of this imagery whose real coherence proceeds from the workings of associative memory.

This quality of Attic imagery emerges vividly when we compare it to the modern comic strip. Where the comic strip propels the narrative through time, juxtaposing images in a determined order, vase painting can only evoke already familiar situations. To borrow from the language of linguistics, the comic strip presents all the images necessary to an understanding of the narrative: we can say that they are there, *in praesentia*, unfolding along a horizontal, or "syntagmatic," axis. On the other hand, the scene depicted on a Greek vase reveals its full meaning only in the framework of an indirect connection, established by the reader's memory, with other scenes figured on other vases. The complementary images are thus absent at the moment of reading, *hic et nunc.* Imagery works *in absentia*, on the vertical or "paradigmatic," axis.

Working from the selection exercised by the painters, we were forced for practical reasons to impose an even more rigorous selection, limiting our choices, at the risk of being misunderstood for lack of illustration, perhaps omitting a nuance here or a supporting document there. The authors of the different chapters of this book have tried to lead the reader, in various ways, to the discovery of this "city of images," the world created by the image-makers.

We may note in passing that it is unusual, at least in the human sciences, for scholars from two different academic institutions to work together on a common project. Most often, doctrinal differences increase the difficulties and each group proceeds alone, often drawn into futile polemics. A long and friendly association has allowed us to surmount such dogmatic obstacles and turn them to creative use. The multiplicity of approaches found in this book is not necessarily a weakness. It enriches our reading of the imagery, varying the angles of attack and emphasizing the plurality of voices. A scene may indeed be examined from different perspectives without yielding contradictory interpretations (cf. figs. 106 and 178). The painters themselves often played on these ambiguities that allow varied approaches. In the ancient world there are numerous examples of objects and monuments interpreted in completely contradictory ways. If the Greek city produced a culture of images, it remains, nevertheless, essentially a culture of the spoken word, of the political and ideological word. Thus the Greeks, as early as the eighth

167

century, began to rediscover the famous Mycenaean tombs and to attribute them to specific kings from Homeric epic in order to reinforce the position of a particular faction in power. In the event of a power shift, the attributions changed without anyone objecting. Here words have more weight than material realities.

It is the same with the imagery. It takes only an inscription imposing a different interpretation from the one to which iconographic logic would have led for a single configuration of imagery to be linked to multiple themes. In fact, the system of imagery, like any system, is closed: the formal combinations are limited in number. For this reason, recourse to language remains the only possible alternative. Here we reach the boundaries between imagery and art. The image-maker, whatever his technical and stylistic virtuosity, is more or less prisoner of a repertoire of grammatical and syntactic elements, figures, and relations out of which he can only make a kind of *bricolage*. The artist, on the other hand, is capable of escaping from this constraining universe and creating his own solutions.

Greece was, as we have said, a civilization of the political word. Politics, however, is conspicuously absent from this book. We have only glimpsed it from time to time, in the world of the warrior, or behind the festival. Equally absent are children and the aged, the sick and the wounded, slaves and courtesans, who only enter into the imagery in order to disappear again just as quickly. Throughout a range of scenes, all the actors are young and beautiful, or mature, athletic, and majestic even in death. Ethnic traits aside, it is at times difficult to recognize a slave or hetaira in this ideal society of interchangeable figures individualized only by an occasional inscribed name. There is scarcely a perceptible difference between two women spinning wool, one capable of giving legitimate children to her husband, and the other a cultivated courtesan.

But we must conclude here, if we are not to begin another book, one that would speak at greater length of women, artisans, and slaves. We would leave the city behind as the image-makers show us scenes of rural life or the world of maritime commerce. Rather than the city of men, we might explore a world of gods and heroes.

Throughout our research we have been fascinated and spurred on by the distance between these scenes and our familiar environment, by their exoticism, which increases the difficulty of reading them, but also by their proximity and their humanity, which involves us and ultimately facilitates our entry into the "city of images."

GLOSSARY

Aegis.   breastplate made of the skin of the goat Amalthea, given to Athena by Zeus; scaly and fringed with snakes, it often has a gorgoneion

Agon.   contest, indicates the spirit of rivalry in competitions

Agonistic.   concerning the agon

Apotropaic.   turning away evil

Aryballos.   elongated vase for perfumed oils

Aulos.   wind instrument, with a vibrating reed, generally used in pairs

Bacchos.   decorated staff carried by candidates for initiation at Eleusis

Bomos.   sacrificial altar

Chiton.   long tunic of very fine pleated fabric

Chlamys.   short coat closed with a fibula

Dinos.   a kind of krater without handles set on a stand

Ephebe.   adolescent; in Athens, specifically designates the age-class from 18 to 20

Erastes.   indicates the adult suitor in a male homosexual relationship

Eromenos.   designates the young beloved in a male homosexual relationship

Flute.   see under aulos; actually an instrument closer to a clarinet or oboe than to our flute

Gorgoneion.   the head of Medusa, the gorgon decapitated by Perseus; used as an apotropaic motif

Gynaeceum.   part of the house reserved for the women

Herm.   stone marker, placed at the crossroads or in front of houses, often in the shape of a head or bust, usually bearded, surmounting a stone pillar marked with the caduceus and representing the god Hermes, most often ithyphallic

Hetaira.   courtesan of rather high social rank, to be distinguished from a prostitute

Hierogamy.   sacred marriage between divinities; a ritual practiced in certain cults

Hieroscopy.   divination by examination of the entrails of the sacrificed victim

Himation.   long coat

Hoplite.   heavily armed foot-soldier whose characteristics are the round shield provided with a central band for the forearm and a grip at the rim

Hydria.   vase used to transport water, with two horizontal handles at the sides and a vertical handle

Ithyphallic.   having an erect penis

Kanoun.   sacrificial basket

Kantharos.   Dionysiac cup with long vertical handles

Komast.   participant in a komos

Komos.   procession of drinkers at a festival, dancing and singing

Krotales.   a kind of castanets used to keep time for the dance

Krypteia.   initiatory period in which adolescents must learn to hide themselves

Lagobolon.   stick used for hunting; shepherd's crook

Lebes.   cauldron, large basin

Lebes gamikos.   vase given as a wedding present

Lekythos.   small vase in the shape of an elongated cylinder with a vertical handle and a narrow neck, used for perfumed oils; often used for funeral rites

Louterion.   stone basin set on a stand

Loutrophoros.   large amphora with a very elongated shape, used to carry water for ritual ablutions

Machaira.   sacrificial knife

Metis.   cunning and calculating intelligence

Nebris.   fawn-skin worn diagonally across the chest

Oenochoe.   wine pitcher, often used in libations

Omphalos.   navel; a stone in the shape of a honey-comb marking a sacred center

Pelike.   a kind of pot-bellied amphora, short and squat

Petasos.   flat hat, with a wide brim

Phiale.   flat cup, without feet, used for libations

Pilos.   felt hat

Pinax.   votive plaque of painted terracotta

Prophylactic.   protecting against misfortune

Psykter.   vase which is floated in the krater to cool the contents

Pyrrhike.   armed dance, invented by Pallas Athena

Pyxis.   small cylindrical box with a cover for jewels or cosmetics

Rhyton.   drinking vase sometimes made of an animal's horn; often has the shape of either a horn or an animal or human head (Dionysos, Silenos, etc.)

Skyphos.   two-handled goblet

Splanchna.   the entrails of the sacrificed animal

Stamnos.   large open vase with horizontal handles, a kind of krater

Strigil.   curved scraper which athletes used to clean their bodies after exercise

Symposium.   drinking-party at which one sings and engages in discussion

Thiasos.   a religious confraternity; Dionysos' retinue

Thyrsos.   rod of fennel surmounted by a pine-cone entwined with ivy or vines

Trapeza.   movable three-legged table

Tympanon.   a kind of tambourine

NOTES ON CONTRIBUTORS

CLAUDE BÉRARD teaches classical archaeology at the University of Lausanne. He has published on the excavations at Eretria (Greece) and on the semiotics of visual imagery (*Anodoi. Recherches sur l'imagerie des passages chthoniens, Bibliotheca Helvetica Romana* 13, Rome, 1974). His most recent publications include *L'héroïsation et la formation de la cité: un conflit idéologique* in *Architecture et Société*, Paris-Rome, 1983, pp. 43ff; "Espace de la cité grecque—espace des imagiers" in the special issue of *Degrés*, Brussels, 35-36, 1983, article C; *Iconographie—Iconologie—Iconologique, Etudes de Lettres*, Lausanne, 1983, fasc. 4, pp. 5ff; *La chasseresse traquée.* Mélanges E. Berger, Basel, 1987.

CHRISTIANE BRON, assistant at the University of Lausanne and holder of a fellowship from the Fonds national de la recherche scientifique, is currently finishing a book with Claude Bérard on *La fête dionysiaque*. A chapter of her thesis has appeared in *Essais sémiotiques, Etudes de Lettres*, Lausanne, 1983, fasc. 4, pp. 39ff, "Chouettes," and another, "La gent ailée d'Athéna Polias," in *L'image en jeux*, Lausanne, 1988.

JEAN-LOUIS DURAND, research fellow at the CNRS, Paris, is engaged in an anthropological investigation of sacrifice in ancient Greece, the preliminary results of which are presented in his book, *Sacrifice et labour en Grèce ancienne*, Paris-Rome, 1986. He collaborated on the collection published by M. Detienne and J.-P. Vernant, *La cuisine du sacrifice en pays grec*, Paris, 1979, and has written, among other articles, with F. Lissarrague, "Les entrailles de la cité," *Hephaistos* 1, 1979, 81ff. and "Un lieu d'image? L'espace du loutérion," *Hephaistos* 2, 1980, 89ff.

FRANÇOISE FRONTISI-DUCROUX, assistant professor at the Collège de France, is the author of *Dédale, mythologie de l'artisan en Grèce ancienne*, Paris, 1975, as well as several articles on Homeric poetry and the rituals of the cults of Artemis. She is currently working on Dionysiac iconography. She is the author of "L'homme, le cerf et le berger. Chemins grecs de la civilité," in *Le Temps de la réflexion* 4, 1983, 53ff. and with J.-P. Vernant, "Figures du masque en Grèce ancienne," *Journal de psychologie* 1983, fasc. 1-2, 53ff. Her most recent publications are *La cithare d'Achille, essai sur la poétique de l'Iliade*, Rome 1986, and "Les limites de l'anthropomorphisme: Hermes et Dionysos" in *Corps des Dieux* (*Le Temps de la Réflexion* VII, 1986).

FRANÇOIS LISSARRAGUE, research fellow at the CNRS, Paris, specializes in Attic imagery. His thesis will appear in 1988 under the title, *L'Autre guerrier; archers, peltastes et cavaliers dans l'imagerie attique.* He has published various articles, notably "Iconographie du Dolon le loup," *Revue archéologique*, 1980, fasc. 1, 3ff. and with A. Schnapp, "Imagerie des Grecs ou Grèce des imagiers?" in *Le temps de la réflexion* 2, 1981, 257ff. He edited, together with F. Thélamon, the Actes du Colloque de Rouen: *Image et céramique grecque*, Université de Rouen, 1983. He has just published *Un flot d'images: une esthétique du banquet grec*, Paris, 1987.

ALAIN SCHNAPP, assistant professor at the Université de Paris I, teaches Greek archaeology. He has taken part in several excavations in Southern Italy and is interested in the historiography and ideology of archaeology. He was the editor of the collection *L'archéologie aujourd'hui*, Paris, 1980. His thesis was published as *Les représentations de la chasse en Grèce ancienne*, Paris, 1973. Among his numerous articles is "Images et programmes: les figurations archaïques de la chasse au sanglier" in *Revue archéologique*, 1979, fasc. 2, 195ff.

JEAN-PIERRE VERNANT, professor at the Collège de France, has profoundly renewed the study of the ancient Greek world by his work founded on anthropology and psychological history. Among his many works, often reprinted and translated into many languages,

171

are *Les origines de la pensée grecque*, Paris, 1962; *Mythe et pensée chez les Grecs*, Paris, 1965 (3rd revised edition 1985); *Mythe et tragédie*, with P. Vidal-Naquet, Paris, 1972; vol. II, Paris, 1986; *Mythe et société*, Paris, 1974; *Les ruses de l'intelligence. La mètis des Grecs*, with M. Detienne, Paris, 1974; *Religions, histoires, raisons*, Paris, 1979; *La mort dans les yeux*, Paris, 1985.

This book served as the guide to a photographic exhibition whose opening coincided with a conference entitled "Images et sociétés en Grèce ancienne: l'iconographie comme méthode d'analyse" (Lausanne, February, 8-11, 1984). The transactions of this conference were published in the Cahiers d'Archéologie Romande, n. 36, Lausanne, 1987.

TABLE OF FIGURES AND ATTRIBUTIONS

1. Milan, Torno coll. C 278. Hydria. *ARV²* 571,73. Early mannerists—Leningrad Painter. 460 B.C.
2. Paris, Louvre F 201. Amphora. *ABV* 274,120. Antimenes Painter. 520 B.C.
3. Oxford, Ashmolean, Cup. Boardman, fig. 177. Manner of the Lysippides Painter. 520/510 B.C.
4. Ferrara, Mus. Naz. T 256B, Kantharos. *ARV²* 266,85 and 971,3. Syriskos Painter. 480 B.C.
5. Ferrara, Mus. Naz. T 256B, Kantharos. *ARV²* 266,85 and 971,3. Syriskos Painter. 480 B.C.
6. London, Brit. Mus. E 765, Askos. *ARV²* 971,3. Class of the Seven Lobster-Claws. 450 B.C.
7. New York, Met. Mus. 38.11.2, Skyphos. *AJA* 43 (1939), figs. 4-7. 480 B.C.
8. New York, Met. Mus. 38.11.2, Skyphos. *AJA* 43 (1939), figs. 4-7. 480 B.C.
9. Bari, Mus. Arch. 3083, Hydria. *ABV* 334,4. A.D. Painter. 520/510 B.C.
10. Paris, Louvre CA 1852, Amphora. *ARV²* 540,4. Near the Boreas Painter. 470 B.C.
11. Adolphseck, 42, Pelike. *ARV²* 285,1. Group of Vienna 895. 470 B.C.
12. Karlsruhe, Bad. Land. Mus. 69/78, Loutrophoros. *ARV²* 1102,2. Manner of the Naples Painter (iii). 440 B.C.
13. Paris, Louvre S 1671, Lebes gamikos. *ARV²* 833,45. Amphitrite Painter. Second quarter 5th century B.C.
14. Paris, Louvre CA 1640, Lekythos. Third quarter 5th century B.C.
15. X-ray photograph of a funerary lekythos. Rouen 1877, *ARV²* 1000, 197. 450 B.C.
16. Berlin, Staatl, Mus. 1930, Oinochoe. *ABV* 573,2. Painter of Half-Palmettes. 490 B.C.
17. Brussels, Musée du Cinquantenaire. A 717, Stamnos. *ARV²* 20,1. Smikros. 510 B.C.
18. Oxford, Ashmolean 523, Stamnos. *ARV²* 621,41. Villa Giulia Painter. 460 B.C.
19. Rome, Vatican Mus., Cup. *ARV²* 427,2. Douris. 500 B.C.
20. Rome, Vatican Mus., Cup. *ARV²* 427,2. Douris. 500 B.C.
21. Ferrara, Mus. Naz. T 128, Krater. *ARV²* 1052,25. Group of Polygnotos. 450 B.C.
22. Berlin, Staatl. Mus. VI 3199, Krater. *ARV²* 1114,9. Hephaistos Painter. 440 B.C.
23. New York, Met. Mus. 27.74, Cup. *ARV²* 407,18. Briseis Painter. 480 B.C.
24. Basel, Antikenmus. Kä 425, Cup. *ARV²* 430,31. Douris. 480 B.C.
25. Paris, Louvre G 355, Krater. *ARV²* 563.10. The Pig-Painter. 460 B.C.
26. London, Brit. Mus. B 174, Amphora. *ABV* 141,1. Near group E: Group of London B 174. 540 B.C.
27. Cambridge, Mass. Fogg Art Mus. 1960.343, Krater. *ARV²* 1042,2. Curti Painter. 440 B.C.
28. Perugia, Mus. Civ., Pelike. Brommer 455 B 4. Beginning of the 4th century B.C.
29. Boston, BFA 01 8024, Cup. *ARV²* 173,9. Ambrosios Painter. 500 B.C.
30. Paris, Louvre G 159, Cup. *ARV²* 413,26. Dokimasia Painter. 480 B.C.
31. Rome, Villa Giulia 50319, Cup. *ARV²* 822,18. Boot Painter. 470 B.C.
32. Copenhagen, Nat. Mus. 6, Cup. *ARV²* 787,3. Dish Painter. 470 B.C.
33. Tarquinia, Mus. Arch. RC 1918, Cup. *ARV²* 366,88. Triptolemos Painter. 480 B.C.
34. Paris, Louvre G 278, Cup. *ARV²* 407,16. Briseis Painter. 480 B.C.
35. Paris, Louvre G 477, Cup. *ARV²* 815,2. Painter of London E 80. 470 B.C.
36. Paris, Louvre G 332, Cup. *ARV²* 396,16. Painter of the Yale Cup. 480 B.C.
37. Rome, Villa Giulia 3590, Cup. *ARV²* 644,129. Providence Painter. 460 B.C.
38. Ex-Rome, Stroganoff. Cup. *ARV²* 415,2. Painter of Agora P 42. 480 B.C.
39. Paris, Louvre G 265, Cup. *ARV²* 416,1. Painter of Louvre G 265. 470 B.C.
40. Berlin, Altes Mus. F 2542, Cup. Blümner pl. 10. 460 B.C.
41. Milan, Mus. Arch. 266, Cup. *ARV²* 379,145. Brygos Painter. 480 B.C.
42. Boston, BFA 01 8033, Cup. *ARV²* 817,14. Telephos Painter. 460 B.C.
43. Paris, Louvre Cp 10994, Cup. *ARV²* 824,23. Orleans Painter. 460 B.C.
44. Altenburg, Staat. Lind. Mus. 229, Cup. *CVA* Altenburg 2, pl. 70. 490 B.C.
45. Boston, MFA 10.184, Cup. *ARV²* 553,39. Pan Painter. 460 B.C.
46. Palermo, private coll., Lekythos. 480 B.C.
47. Berlin, Staat. Mus. 4560, Pelike. *ARV²* 246. Near the Painter of the Munich Amphora. 490 B.C.
48. Paris, Louvre G 278, Cup. *ARV²* 407,16. Briseis Painter. 480 B.C.
49. Berlin, Staat. Mus. 2268, Cup. *ARV²* 153,2. Painter of Berlin 2268. 500 B.C.
50. Paris, Louvre G 37, Cup. *ARV²* 113,5. Thalia Painter. 510 B.C.
51. Paris, Louvre G 292, Cup. *ARV²* 345,71. Manner of the Antiphon Painter. 480 B.C.
52. Paris, BN 523, Cup. *ARV²* 316,4. Proto-Panaetion Group. 490 B.C.
53. Berlin, Staat. Mus. 2307, Cup. *ARV²* 341,77. Antiphon Painter. 490 B.C.
54. Paris, Louvre G 136, Cup. *ARV²* 231,78. Eucharides Painter. 490 B.C.
55. Paris, Louvre G 102, Oinochoe. *ARV²* 156,52. Painter of Berlin 2268. 500 B.C.
56. Pontecagnano, Mus. Arch. T 1240, Oinochoe, unpublished. Painter of Berlin 2268. 500 B.C.
57. Heidelberg, University 71/1, Oinochoe. *ARV²* 156,54. Painter of Berlin 2268. 500 B.C.
58. Cambridge, Fitzwilliam Mus. 37.18, Cup. *ARV²* 231,76. Eucharides Painter. 490 B.C.
59. Paris, Louvre G 22, Cup. *ARV²* 151,52. Near the Epeleios Painter. 500 B.C.
60. Paris, Louvre CA 2192, Oinochoe. *ARV²* 983,14. Class of the Owl-Skyphoi. 480 B.C.
61. London, Brit. Mus. E 448, Stamnos. *ARV²* 992,65. Achilles Painter. 450 B.C.
62. Tübingen, University E 104, Krater. *ARV²* 603,35. Niobid Painter. 460 B.C.
63. Munich, Staat. Ant. 2307, Amphora. *ARV²* 26,1. Euthymides. 520 B.C.
64. Rome, Capitol. Mus. 88, Amphora. *ABV* 270,66. Antimenes Painter. 520 B.C.
65. Würzburg, Martin v. Wagner Mus. L 199, Amphora. *ABV* 287,5. Group of Würzburg 199. 520 B.C.
66. Ferrara, Mus. Naz. T 740, Krater. *ARV²* 599,6. Niobid Painter. 460 B.C.
67. Cambridge, Fitzwilliam Mus. G 140, Lekythos. *ARV²* 1008,3. Loosely connected with the Achilles Painter's white lekythoi. 450 B.C.
68. Würzburg, Martin v. Wagner Mus. L 507, Amphora. *ARV²* 181.1 Kleophrades Painter. Last quarter 6th c.—510.
69. Florence, Mus. Arch. 4209, Krater. *ABV* 76,1. Kleitias. 570 B.C.
70. Munich, Staat. Ant. 1470, Amphora. *ABV* 144,6. Exekias. 540 B.C.
71. Paris, Louvre F 201, Amphora. *ABV* 274,120. Antimenes Painter. 520 B.C.
72. Paris, Louvre G 179, Hydria. Pottier III, pl. 126. 470 B.C.
73. Ferrara, Mus. Naz. T 416 B VP, Krater. *ARV²* 1144,21. Kleophon Painter. 440 B.C.
74. Rome, Villa Giulia, Ionian Hydria. *ASAA* 24-26, pp. 47-57. 540 B.C.
75. Berlin, Staat. Mus. F 1915, Olpe. *ABV* 377,247. Group of Leagros. 520 B.C.
76. Warsaw, Nat. Mus. 142464, Cup-Skyphos. *ARV²* 797,142. Euaion Painter. 480 B.C.
77. Paris, Louvre G 402, Oinochoe. *ARV²* 1214,2. Kraipale Painter. 430 B.C.
78. Paris, Louvre C 10918, Cup. *ARV²* 467,130. Makron. 490 B.C.
79. Series of drawings, all by the Gela Painter—490/480 B.C., from left to right:
London, Brit. Mus. 1905.7-11.1, Oinochoe. *ABV* 475,29.
Athens, Nat. Mus. 18568, Lekythos. Para. 216.

Tübingen, Univ. 5738, Lekythos. *ABL* 209,78.

Amsterdam, Allard Pierson 8196, Lekythos. *ABL* 209,96.

Athens, Agora P 24067, Lekythos. *ABV* 715, 16ter.

Naples, Mus. Naz. 81190, Lekythos. *ABL* 207,46.

Basel market, Lekythos. *MM* Sale 51,136.

Basel market, Oinochoe. *MM* Liste. R.37.

Amsterdam, Allard Pierson 268, Lekythos. BABesch 49.

80. Heidelberg, Univ. 253, Olpe. *CVA*, Deut. 10, pl. 39. 520 B.C.

81. Boston, BFA 99.538, Amphora. *ABV* 255,6. Lysippides Painter. 530 B.C.

82. Boston, BFA 95.25, Krater. *ARV²* 1149,9. Manner of the Kleophon Painter. 440 B.C.

83. Viterbo, Museo, Amphora, *Bolletino d'Arte* 29, 1985, 1-16. Group E. 540 B.C.

84. Berlin, Staat. Mus. 1900, Hydria. *ABV* 385,27. Acheloos Painter. 520 B.C.

85. Athens, Nat. Mus. 3036, Lekythos, unpublished. 450 B.C.

86. Karlsruhe, Bad. Land. Mus. 85/1. Lekythos. *ARV²* 685,164. Bowdoin Painter. 470 B.C.

87. Orvieto, Mus. Faina 722, Cup. SE 34, pl. 8a. 530 B.C.

88. Oxford, Ashmolean 1889.1013, Lekythos. *ABL* 262,1. Manner of the Athena Painter. 500 B.C.

89. Rome, Villa Giulia 50543, Cup. Mingazzini, no. 627, pl. 98, 2-3. 520 B.C.

90. Leiden, Rijksmus. PC 63, Hydria. *ABV* 266,1. Antimenes Painter. 520 B.C.

91. London, Brit. Mus. B 304, Hydria. *ABV* 266,4. Antimenes Painter. 520 B.C.

92. Basel, private coll., Amphora. Para. 187,3. Painter of Vatican 342. 520 B.C.

93. Paris, Louvre G 623, Cup. *ARV²* 1294. Near the Painter of London E 105. 440 B.C.

94. Paris, Louvre G 637, Cup. *ARV²* 770,5. Related to the Sotades Painter. 460 B.C.

95. Rome, Vatican 16548, Hydria. *ARV²* 179,3. Carpenter Painter. 500 B.C.

96. Baltimore, Walters Art Gal. 48.21.15, Cup. *ARV²* 336,16. Antiphon Painter. 490 B.C.

97. Ferrara, Mus. Naz. T 136 VP, Krater. *CVA*, Italy 37, pl. 13. 410 B.C.

98. Paris, Louvre G 343, Krater. *ARV²* 600,17. Niobid Painter. 460 B.C.

99. London, Brit. Mus. B 678, Phiale. *AK*, Suppl. 7. pl. 19,3. 520 B.C.

100. Brussels, Musée du Cinquantenaire, R 343, Skyphos. *CVA* Belg. 2, pl. 20,1. 500 B.C.

101. Rome, Villa Giulia 74966, Skyphos. *NS*, pl. 59. 500 B.C.

102. Bollingen, private coll., Cup. Ant. Kunst, pl. 17. 540/530 B.C.

103. Vienna, Kunsthist. Mus. 194, Lekythos. *ABL* 216,3. Edinburgh Painter. 510 B.C.

104. London, Brit. Mus. B 421, Cup. *ABV* 181.1. Tleson. 540 B.C.

105. London, Brit. Mus. B 52, Olpe. *ABV* 153,31. Amasis Painter. 540 B.C.

106. Munich, Staat. Ant. 8763, Amphora. Para. 65. Amasis Painter. 550 B.C.

107. Athens, Kerameikos 6159, Lekythos. *ABV* 58,127. c Painter. 560 B.C.

108. Paris, Louvre A 479, Cup. *ABV* 156,80. Amasis Painter. 550 B.C.

109. Paris, Louvre F 85 bis, Cup. *CVA*, France 8, pl. 79,6. 540 B.C.

110. Boston, MFA 08.291. Lekythos. *ABV* 92. Painter of Boston 08.291. 550 B.C.

111. London, Brit. Mus. D 60, Lekythos. *ARV²* 1230,37. Thanatos Painter. 440 B.C.

112. Athens, Kerameikos 2713, Alabastron. Para. 331. 500 B.C.

113. Rome, Villa Giulia 50462, Amphora. *ARV²* 284,3. Matsch Painter. 490 B.C.

114. Munich, Staat. Ant. 2655, Cup. *ARV²* 471,196. Makron. 480 B.C.

115. Berlin, Staat. Mus. 2291, Cup. *ARV²* 459,4. Makron. 490 B.C.

116. Tarquinia, 701, Cup. *ARV²* 348,4. Cage Painter. 490 B.C.

117. Gotha, Mus. Ahv 48, Cup. *ARV²* 20. Last quarter 6th c.–520.

118. Küsnacht, Private coll. 33, Cup. Hirchmann. Douris. 490 B.C.

119. Laon, Musée 37.1056, Cup. *ARV²* 874,4. Ancona Painter. 460 B.C.

120. Brussels, Musée du Cinquantenaire, A 2323, Kyathos. *ARV²* 333,2. Oinophile Painter. 500 B.C.

121. London, Brit. Mus. E 46, Cup. *ARV²* 315,1. Proto-Panaetion Group. 500 B.C.

122. Copenhagen, Nat. Mus. 14268, Cup. *ARV²* 1583,2. 500 B.C.

123. New York, Met. Mus. 31.11.10, Lekythos. *ABV* 154,57. Amasis Painter. 550 B.C.

124. Lausanne, private coll., Hydria. 460 B.C.

125. Vienna, Kunsthist. Mus. I 6788, Krater. 420 B.C.

126. Küsnacht, private coll., Skyphos. 460/450 B.C.

127. Bari, Mus. Civ. 4979, Krater. *ARV²* 236,4. Akin to Göttingen Painter. 490 B.C.

128. Rome, Villa Giulia 2609, Amphora. Para. 146,8ter. Priam Painter. 520 B.C.

129. Compiègne, Mus. Vivenel 1090, Cup. *ARV²* 922,1. Wedding Painter. 460 B.C.

130. Rome, Vatican 417, Hydria. *ABV* 384,26. Acheloos Painter. 520 B.C.

131. Karlsruhe, Bad. Land. Mus., Lekythos. *CVA*, Deut. 7, pl. 27. 390 B.C.

132. Paris, Louvre CA 1679, Lebes fragment. *ARV²* 1179,3. Painter of Athens 1454. 400 B.C.

133. London, Brit. Mus. E 241, Hydria. *ARV²* 1482,1. Apollonia Group. 380 B.C.

134. Leningrad, Hermitage 928, Lekythos. *ARV²* 1482,6. Apollonia Group. 380 B.C.

135. Basel market, Krater. *MM*, Auction 63, n. 26. 520/510 B.C.

136. Paris, Louvre CP 11269, Krater. *CVA*, France 12, pl. 166. 520 B.C.

137. New York, Met. Mus. 56.11.1, Lekythos. Para. 66. Amasis Painter. 540 B.C.

138. Athens, Nat. Mus. 1630, Pyxis. Licht, pl. 173. 380 B.C.

139. Copenhagen, Nat. Mus. 9080, Loutrophoros. *ARV²* 841,75. Sabouroff Painter. 460 B.C.

140. Paris, Louvre CA 587, Pyxis. *ARV²* 1094,104. Painter of Louvre Centauromachy. 450 B.C.

141. Paris, Louvre CA 1857, Pyxis. 430 B.C.

142. Basel, *MM* Auction XIV, n. 61, Pinax. 510 B.C.

143. Paris, Louvre CA 453, Loutrophoros. *ARV²* 184,22. Kleophrades Painter. 550 B.C.

144. Athens, Nat. Mus. 450, Loutrophoros. *CVA*, Greece 1, pls. 8-9. 500 B.C.

145. Paris, BN 355, Kantharos. *ABV* 346,8. Class of the One-Handled Kantharoi. 510 B.C.

146. Paris, BN 353, Kantharos. *ABV* 346,7. Class of the One-Handled Kantharoi. 510 B.C.

147. Athens, Nat. Mus. 1821, Lekythos. *ARV²* 998,168. Achilles Painter. 460 B.C.

148. Munich, Staat. Ant. 2797, Lekythos. *ARV²* 1022,138. Phiale Painter. 450 B.C.

149. Athens, Nat. Mus. 1759, Lekythos. *ARV²* 1376,1. Reed Painter. 420 B.C.

150. Athens, Nat. Mus. 1926, Lekythos. *ARV²* 846,193. Sabouroff Painter. 460 B.C.

151. Münster, Arch. Mus. 24, Lekythos. 500 B.C.

152. Basel, *MM* Auktion XVIII, n. 85, Cup. 540 B.C.

153. Berlin, Staat. Mus. 1686, Amphora. *ABV* 296,4. Painter of Berlin 1686. 540 B.C.

154. Uppsala, Gustavianum 352, Hydria. *ABV* 519,15. Theseus Painter. 500 B.C.

155. Paris, BN 243, Amphora. 530 B.C.

156. Copenhagen, Nat. Mus. Chr. VIII 340, Oinochoe. *CVA*, Danmark 3, pl. 122. 510 B.C.

157. London, Sotheby's Sale Dec. 1982, n. 239, Cup. 490 B.C.

158. Eleusis, Arch. Mus. 636, Stamnos. *ARV²* 1052,23. Group of Polygnotos. 450 B.C.

159. New York, Met. Mus. 28.57.23, Krater. *ARV²* 1012,1. Persephone Painter. 450 B.C.

160. Brussels, Musée du Cinquantenaire, A 10, Skyphos. *ARV²* 661,86. Painter of the Yale Lekythos. 470 B.C.

161. Athens, Nat. Mus. 11036, Pinax. 380 B.C.

162. Athens, Nat. Mus. 17297, Hydria. Metzger, pl. 19. 360 B.C.
163. Paris, Louvre G 343, Krater. *ARV²* 600,17. Niobid Painter. 460 B.C.
164. Berlin, Staat. Mus. F 2173, Pelike. *ARV²* 286,18. Geras Painter. 480 B.C.
165. Berlin, Staat. Mus. F 2173, Pelike. *ARV²* 286,18. Geras Painter. 480 B.C.
166. Rome, Villa Giulia 983, Stamnos. *ARV²* 621,33. Villa Giulia Painter. 460 B.C.
167. Paris, Louvre G 227, Pelike. *ARV²* 283,2. Painter of Louvre G 238. 480 B.C.
168. Copenhagen, Nat. Mus. 3836, Krater. *ARV²* 241,48. Myson. 500 B.C.
169. Copenhagen, Nat. Mus. 3836, Krater. *ARV²* 241,48. Myson. 500 B.C.
170. Berlin, Staat. Mus. F 2309, Cup. Para. 372,11 bis. Dokimasia Painter. 480 B.C.
171. London, Brit. Mus. E 768, Psykter. *ARV²* 446,262. Douris. 490 B.C.
172. Paris, Louvre G 133, Cup. *ARV²* 348,7. Cage Painter. 490 B.C.
173. Geneva, Mus. Art et Hist. 16908, Cup. *CVA*, Switz. I, pl. 9. 500 B.C.
174. Brussels, Musée du Cinquantenaire A 717, Stamnos. *ARV²* 20,1. Smikros. 510 B.C.
175. Berlin, Staat. Mus. 3155, Krater. *ARV²* 585,25. Earlier mannerists. 460 B.C.
176. Athens, Nat. Mus. 1357, Cup. *MDAI(A)* 9, pl. 1. 490/480 B.C.
177. Paris, Louvre G 185, Stamnos. *ARV²* 207,142. Berlin Painter. 500 B.C.
178. Munich, Staat. Ant. 8763, Amphora. Para. 65. Amasis Painter. 540 B.C.
179. Paris, Louvre F 36, Amphora. *ABV* 150,6. Amasis Painter. 550 B.C.
180. Florence, Mus. Arch. 4209, Krater. *ABV* 76,1. Kleitias. 570 B.C.
181. Chiusi, Mus. Arch. 1830, Skyphos. *ARV²* 975,36. Lewis Painter. 460 B.C.
182. Paris, Louvre AM 1008, Amphora. 540 B.C.
183. Rome, Villa Giulia 2609, Amphora. Para. 146,8ter. Priam Painter. 520 B.C.
184. Munich, Staat. Ant. 1562, Amphora. 520 B.C.
185. Ferrara, Mus. Naz. T 254 C VP, Krater. *ARV²* 524,26. Orchard Painter. 460 B.C.
186. Bologna, Mus. Civ. 241, Krater. *ARV²* 524,25. Orchard Painter. 460 B.C.
187. Paris, Louvre E 876, Dinos. *ABV* 90,1. Painter of Louvre E 876. 560 B.C.
188. Würzburg, Martin v. Wagner Mus. HA 166a, Krater. *CVA*, Deut. 39, pl. 44. 510 B.C.
189. Taranto, Mus. Naz. 20319, Krater. *ARV²* 234,5. Göttingen Painter. 490 B.C.
190. Athens, Nat. Mus. A 498, Skyphos. *CVA*, Greece 1, pl. 4. 500 B.C.
191. Munich, Staat. Ant. 2390, Krater. *ARV²* 1456,3. L.C. Group. 350 B.C.
192. London, Brit. Mus. E 532, Oinochoe. 430 B.C.
193. Tarquinia, Mus. Naz. RC 4197, Krater. *ARV²* 1057,96. Group of Polygnotos. 450 B.C.
194. Paris, Louvre G 532, Stamnos. *CVA*, France 4, pl. 21. 440 B.C.
195. Naples, Mus. Naz. 3240, Krater. *ARV²* 1336,1. Pronomos Painter. 410 B.C.
196. Munich, Staat. Ant. 2657, Cup. *ARV²* 475,267. Makron. 490 B.C.
197. London, Brit. Mus. E 790, Rhyton. *ARV²* 1550,1. Close to the Persian class. 430 B.C.
198. Korinth, Amer. Sch., Cup. *ARV²* 1519,13. Q Painter. 390 B.C.
199. Florence, Mus. Arch. 3914, Cup. *ARV²* 769,4. Painter of Florence 3968. 450 B.C.
200. Oxford, Ashmolean 1924.2, Cup. *ARV²* 865,1. Painter of Athens 1237. 450 B.C.
201. Copenhagen, Nat. Mus. ABC 1021, Krater. *ARV²* 1035,2. Group of Bologna PU 289. 440 B.C.
202. Paris, BN 576, Cup. *ARV²* 371,14. Brygos Painter. 480 B.C.
203. Bologna, Mus. Civ. 283, Krater. *ARV²* 1151,1. Dinos Painter. 430 B.C.
204. Paris, BN 357, Amphora. *ARV²* 987,2. Achilles Painter. 450 B.C.
205. London, Brit. Mus. E 439, Stamnos. *ARV²* 298. 450 B.C.
206. Berlin, Staat. Mus. 2290, Cup. *ARV²* 462,48. Makron. 490 B.C.

207. Berlin, Staat. Mus. 2290, Cup. *ARV²* 462,48. Makron. 490 B.C.
208. Boulogne, Musée 559, Cup. *AK,* Suppl. 6, pl. 16,1. 510 B.C.
209. Athens, private coll., Oinochoe. *ARV²* 1249,13. Eretria Painter. 420 B.C.
210. Berlin, Staat. Mus. 1930, Oinochoe. *ABV* 573,2. Painter of Half-Palmettes. 490 B.C.
211. New York, Met. Mus. 75.2.21, Lekythos. *ABL* 222,27. Marathon Painter. 490 B.C.
212. Palermo, Mus. Arch. 20.23, Lekythos. *ABL* 206,3. Gela Painter. 490 B.C.
213. Paris, Louvre F 131, Cup. *ABV* 206,3. Group of Walters 48.62. 520 B.C.
214. Tarquinia, Mus. Naz. RC 1804, Amphora. *ABV* 275,5. Class of neck-amphorae with masks. 520 B.C.
215. Paris, Louvre F 130, Cup. *ABV* 262,49. Lysippides Painter. 510 B.C.
216. Paris, BN 277, Lekythos. *CVA*, France 7, pl. 46. 540 B.C.
217. Copenhagen, Ny Carlsberg 3385, Cup. Para. 104. Segment Class. 510 B.C.
218. Naples, Mus. Naz. 81146, Cup. *CVA*, Italy 20, pl. 32. 520 B.C.
219. London, Brit. Mus. E 180, Hydria. *ARV²* 218. 500 B.C.
220. Cleveland, Mus. of Art 76.89, Cup. *ARV²* 7,7. Psiax. 510 B.C.
221. Melbourne, Nat. Gal. 1730.4, Cup. *ARV²* 125,20. Nikosthenes Painter. 510 B.C.
222. Basel, Antikenmus., Cup. *MDAI(A)* 90, pl. 35,1. 490 B.C.
223. London, Brit. Mus. E 78, Cup. *ARV²* 401,3. Foundry Painter. 480 B.C.
224. Rome, Villa Giulia, Cup. *ARV²* 1623,66 bis. Oltos. 520 B.C.
225. Florence, Mus. Arch. 4209, Krater. *ABV* 76,1. Kleitias. 570 B.C.
226. Munich, Staat. Ant. WAF 2088, Cup. *ABV* 232. 520 B.C.
227. London, Brit. Mus. E 64, Cup. *ARV²* 455,9. Ashby Painter. 490 B.C.
228. Paris, Louvre G 133, Cup. *ARV²* 348,7. Cage Painter. 490 B.C.
229. Copenhagen, Nat. Mus. 3880, Cup. Para. 372,11ter. Dokimasia Painter. 480 B.C.
230. Cambridge, Fitzwilliam Mus. 61, Cup. *ABV* 202,2. Painter of Cambridge 61. 510 B.C.
231. London, Brit. Mus. B 376, Mastos. Fest. Brommer, pl. 39. 510 B.C.

ABBREVIATIONS

ABL	Haspels, E. *Attic Black-figured Lekythoi,* 1936.
ABV	J. D. Beazley, *Attic Black-Figure Vase-Painters,* Oxford, 1956.
AJA	*American Journal of Archeology.*
AK	*Antike Kunst.*
Ant. Kunst	*Antike Kunst aus Privatbesitz: Bern, Biel, Solothurn,* 1967.
ARV²	J. D. Beazley, *Attic Red-Figure Vase-Painters,* Oxford, 1963.
ASAA	*Annuario della Scuola Archeologica di Atene.*
BABesch	*Bulletin van de Vereeniging tot bevordering der Kennis van de antieke Beschaving.*
Blümner	*Technologie II,* 1912.
Boardman	*Attic Black-Figure Vases,* London, 1974.
Brommer	*Vasenlisten III,* 1973.
CVA	*Corpus Vasorum Antiquorum.*
Fest. Brommer	*Festschrift für F. Brommer,* 1977.
JHS	*Journal of Hellenic Studies.*
Licht	*Sittengeschichte Griechenlands II,* 1926.
MDAI(A)	*Mitteilungen des Deutschen Archäologischen Instituts, Athens.*
Metzger	*Recherches sur l'imagerie athénienne,* 1965.
Mingazzini	*Vasi della collezione Castallani,* 1930.
MM	*Münzen und Medaillen,* auction catalogue, Basel.
NS	*Nuove scoperte e acquisizioni nell'Etruria meridionale,* ed. E. Nardini, 1975.
Para.	J. D. Beazley, *Paralipomena, Addition to ABV and ARV,* Oxford, 1971.
Pottier	*Vases antiques du Louvre III,* 1922.
SE	*Studi etruschi.*

ILLUSTRATION CREDITS

ACKNOWLEDGMENTS

This book was conceived on the occasion of the travelling exhibit of the same name, for which it takes the place of a catalogue. We wish to extend our warmest thanks to those who helped make this two-fold project a reality—in France, the *Centre national de la recherche scientifique*; the *Ministère des relations extérieures* and the *Association française d'action artistique*; the *Ministère des affaires culturelles* and the *Direction régionale d'Ile-de-France*; in Switzerland—the *Service des affaires culturelles* of the *Municipalité de Lausanne*; the *Commission cantonale vaudoise de la formation culturelle*; the *Société académique vaudoise*; the *Université de Lausanne* and the *Faculté des lettres*.

In addition to these organizations which gave us their official support, we are happy to be able to express our gratitude to the following companies which generously underwrote the project—La Bâloise, Compagnie d'assurances, Lausanne; Banque Cantonale Vaudoise; Banque de Dépôts et de Gestion, Lausanne; Bobst SA, Lausanne; Chanel Parfums, Paris; Charles Veillon SA, Lausanne; Crédit Foncier Vaudois; Kodak SA, Lausanne; Kodak-Pathé, Paris; Nestlé SA, Vevey; Philip Morris, Lausanne; Publicitas SA, Lausanne; and several anonymous donors.

Thanks also to all the specialists who offered us their expertise—Baumgartner Papiers SA, Crissier; l'Imprimerie Bron SA, and in particular M. Fasoletti; the photographers A. Chéné (Centre Camille Jullian, CNRS); G. Fankhauser, Villars-Sainte-Croix; U. and A. Held, Ecublens; J. Bernal, draughtsman at the *Institut d'archéologie et d'histoire ancienne de l'Université de Lausanne*; M. Cuendet, director of the *Atelier des maquettes* of the city of Lausanne; F. Bolli and C. Spillmann, decorators; P.-A. Mottier and the colleagues of the *Institut d'archéologie et d'histoire ancienne*.

We also wish to thank our museum colleagues and friends—I. Aghion, B. d'Agostino, J.-C. Balty, H. A. Cahn, H.-P. Isler, A. Pasquier, M. Schmidt, B. Tailliez, G. Sennequier, D. J. R. Williams. We wish to express our appreciation to Robert Guy for his advice during the preparation of the American edition, and finally, to our translator Deborah Lyons, for her care and patience.

Library of Congress Cataloging-in-Publication Data

Cité des images. English.
A city of images: iconography and society in Ancient Greece/Claude Bérard...
et al.; translated by Deborah Lyons.
p.   cm.
Translation of: Cité des images.
Bibliography: p.
ISBN 0-691-03591-1 (alk paper):
1. Athens (Greece)–Antiquities–Exhibitions.
2. Greece–Antiquities–Exhibitions.
3. Pottery, Greek–Greece–Athens–Exhibitions.
4. Greece–Religious life and customs–Exhibitions.
5. Greece–Social life and customs–Exhibitions.
I. Bérard, Claude. II. Title
DF275.C3613   1988
938'.5–DC 19   88-22664
CIP